from fear to facebook

One School's Journey

Matt Levinson

D1057112

International Society for Technology in Education
EUGENE, OREGON • WASHINGTON, DC

from fear to facebook
One School's Journey
Matt Levinson

Director of Book Publishing: *Courtney Burkholder*
Acquisitions Editor: *Jeff V. Bolkan*
Production Editors: *Tina Wells, Lynda Gansel*
Production Coordinator: *Rachel Williams*
Graphic Designer: *Signe Landin*
Copy Editor: *Beth Ina*
Proofreader: *Kathy Hamman*
Cover Design, Book Design, and Production: *Kim McGovern*

Library of Congress Cataloging-in-Publication Data

Levinson, Matt.
  From fear to facebook : one school's journey / Matt Levinson. — 1st ed.
    p. cm.
  ISBN 978-1-56484-270-1 (pbk.)
  1. Instructional systems—Design. 2. Computer-assisted instruction.
  3. Educational technology. I. International Society for Technology in Education. II. Title.
  LB1028.38.L48 2010
  371.33'44678—dc22

                                                                    2010009738

First Edition
ISBN: 978-1-56484-270-1
Printed in the United States of America

ISTE® is a registered trademark of the International Society for Technology in Education.

SUSTAINABLE FORESTRY INITIATIVE Certified Fiber Sourcing
Label applies to the text stock www.sfiprogram.org

About ISTE

The International Society for Technology in Education (ISTE) is the trusted source for professional development, knowledge generation, advocacy, and leadership for innovation. ISTE is the premier membership association for educators and education leaders engaged in improving teaching and learning by advancing the effective use of technology in PK–12 and teacher education.

Home of the National Educational Technology Standards (NETS) and ISTE's annual conference and exposition (formerly known as NECC), ISTE represents more than 100,000 professionals worldwide. We support our members with information, networking opportunities, and guidance as they face the challenge of transforming education. To find out more about these and other ISTE initiatives, visit our website at www.iste.org.

As part of our mission, ISTE Book Publishing works with experienced educators to develop and produce practical resources for classroom teachers, teacher educators, and technology leaders. Every manuscript we select for publication is carefully peer-reviewed and professionally edited. We value your feedback on this book and other ISTE products. E-mail us at books@iste.org.

Contact Us

International Society for Technology in Education (ISTE)
Washington, DC, Office:
 1710 Rhode Island Ave. NW, Suite 900, Washington, DC 20036-3132
Eugene, Oregon, Office:
 180 West 8th Ave., Suite 300, Eugene, OR 97401-2916
Order Desk: 1.800.336.5191
Order Fax: 1.541.302.3778
Customer Service: orders@iste.org
Book Publishing: books@iste.org
Book Sales and Marketing: booksmarketing@iste.org
Web: www.iste.org

About the Author

 A graduate of Haverford College and Teachers' College, Columbia University, **Matt Levinson** has worked in schools for 17 years, as a middle and high school history teacher, dean of students, department chair, and middle school division head. He is currently the head of the middle school at the Nueva School in Hillsborough, California.

Dedication

This book is dedicated to my wife, Pri, for her unwavering support, sense of humor, and encouragement and to my children, Sanjay and Maya, for their endless inspiration every day.

Acknowledgments

I would like to thank my parents and my sister for their faithful reading of the book from start to finish and their continuous words of support. My former Princeton Day School colleague George Sanderson proved to be a dedicated reader and provided important feedback and encouragement.

Diane Rosenberg championed my writing from the beginning and provided many hours of humor and good cheer through the project. I would also like to thank my colleagues at Nueva for their inspiration in always looking for innovative ways to work with students with technology. Finally, I would like to thank the Nueva students for teaching me new ways of looking at and imagining the world with technology.

In the Nueva tech office, I'd like to thank Diana Nemirovsky and her team for helping with the first year rollout of the laptop program. Her humor, responsiveness, technical guidance, and expertise helped me, the students, and the school figure out the initial landscape of the 1-to-1 laptop program.

At ISTE, I would like to thank Jeff Bolkan for his initial editing and review of the book and his support through the revision and rewriting process. Also, Tina Wells proved to be instrumental in her review of the book, from revisions to the galleys. Megan Dolman also was very helpful with the rollout of the book. I appreciate their continued support of the project; and they were all great to work with through the process.

Contents

Best-laid plans aren't necessarily successful plans! Our ambitious 1-to-1 rollout didn't go as smoothly as we'd hoped. Even with lessons learned, we found more surprises and challenges in the second year.

Middle school students are social; thus, it is no surprise that they view technology as a social tool. We strove to find a working balance between the needs and work styles of students and the security and learning needs of the school.

Just as iTunes has changed the way we consume music by making custom playlists available, ubiquitous computing offers schools the opportunity to customize learning for each student.

Again, balancing safety and access is a tricky task, and some of the solutions involve thorny ethical dilemmas. To protect kids, do we really want to encourage them to lie about who they are online?

Contents

foreword

Think about the different times you've gathered the courage to try something new. Perhaps you are like me and have memories of climbing that never-ending ladder of the high diving board. You probably had already dived off the smaller board numerous times, but this was the first time you mustered enough courage to try something new. Eventually, you just closed your eyes and jumped.

Our education system is in the midst of a paradigm shift, where new methods, environments, and assessment models need to be acquired if schools are to keep pace with our increasingly networked culture. As the conversation about the digital divide shifts from questions of technological access to ones concerning participation, educators must work to ensure that every young person has access to the tools, skills, and experiences needed to join in this new participatory culture.

Today's educators have a chance to be courageous and take the risk of jumping off the high dive. Those who do so will give students opportunities to bring their passions into the classroom and encourage them to gain the cultural competencies and social skills they will need in their future roles as 21st-century citizens and workers. Whereas the industrial age prepared many to be workers on assembly lines, today's information age challenges us to be critical thinkers and active citizens, to come together collectively and conceptualize solutions to new problems that didn't exist in the last decade.

More schools in the United States are adopting 1-to-1 laptop initiatives. Evidence indicates that these programs produce improved student achievement and motivation. The laptops support a more interdisciplinary approach to learning in which teachers and students can work together to create projects. The 1-to-1 initiative offers new forms of communication between teachers and students and creates a transparent space where the larger community of parents and administrators can become more involved and aware of learning taking place in the school (*Laptops for Learning, Final Report and Recommendations of the Laptops for Learning Task Force,* March 22, 2004).

We can learn about opportunities in Matt Levinson's *From Fear to Facebook: One School's Journey,* the story of how Nueva School established a 1-to-1 laptop initiative. What's apparent in this school's story is the realization that it is not the technology that makes a 1-to-1 laptop initiative a success but knowing how to use media and technology effectively in the classroom, while knowing not to put technology first or have it replace the important, necessary teacher–student relationship and the community that supports each child's learning experience.

When starting the laptop initiative, Nueva School planners didn't take the traditional route of phasing in 1-to-1 laptops one grade at a time. Instead, they recognized the critical technological juncture of society and the need for speed in addressing it. Consider the new technology and practices that have emerged in the past five years alone ... YouTube, Wikipedia, Facebook, Machinima, Crowdsourcing, and Trending. Change is happening at lightning speed, and if educators respond to it at a turtle's pace, we run the risk of failing to prepare a generation of our future workforce for jobs that don't exist today but will tomorrow, jobs that require citizens to be engaged, think critically, and act together.

From Fear to Facebook provides a map of the promises and perils of launching a 1-to-1 laptop program all at once in a middle school and shows how the Nueva School has lived up to its school motto, "Learn by Doing; Learn by Caring." This motto perfectly describes the process of learning in a participatory culture.

A participatory culture is one that has relatively low barriers to engagement, offers strong support for creating and sharing, provides some type of informal mentorship and a degree of social connection, and instills in its members the belief that their contributions matter (*Confronting the Challenges of Participatory Culture: Media Education in the 21st Century*, 2006). Infusing this type of culture in the Nueva School encouraged administrators, parents, teachers, and students alike to embrace media in learning and see its intrinsic pedagogical value.

I've had the good fortune of visiting Nueva and spending time with its teachers and students. This community comes together to encourage students to be critical thinkers. The students have the ability to create meaning, and this was obvious in every class I visited.

Nueva School provides various modes of professional development to support teachers in developing new opportunities that build on the 1-to-1 laptop initiative. When I sat in on the fifth grade Social and Emotional Learning (SEL) class, we each playfully put one foot on the table and traced the outline of our shoe as we began the process of brainstorming about what a digital footprint might include. As we shared our footprints with each other, students shouted out the names of informative websites, engaging games, and virtual networks they loved to visit. Students shared the places that connected them to their passions, and the teacher facilitated a discussion on what it means to be socially responsible "citizens" online in the spaces that matter to them. This interdisciplinary approach helps to nurture the whole child.

You might expect that a class called Social and Emotional Learning would foster such healthy dialogue, but it soon became obvious in every class I visited that the Nueva School as a whole seizes opportunities to create shared dialogues where administrators, students, teachers, parents, and visitors feel welcome and are encouraged to offer their opinions and add to the conversation.

One of the key principles that emerges in this book is the old proverb, "It takes a village to raise a child." When you create a learning environment that asks the current walls of the "learning garden" to break down and be porous, then you're bound to have controversy, because parents exhibit many different values in rearing their children. Parents often break into two camps on the issue of connecting children to the world outside of the school walls. One side would like to have less restriction and provide students the freedom to explore, while the other side would rather have more restrictions put in place.

When thinking about integrating technology into the classroom, I am one of those parents who envisions this as an opportunity, a situation in which the glass is half full. We cannot continue to create barriers that separate school from home, home from work, and work from community. Technology has produced a domino effect in which each of these is interconnected in one community. This became obvious at the Nueva School as it struggled with creating laptop policies and as students' laptop use spilled into the home and outside of class time.

Although many articles introduce excellent examples of teachers and students doing innovative projects, such instances are actually sporadic and widely separated throughout the United States. Currently, there is a tension between the desire to instill a culture of participatory learning and schools' practice of providing a "one size fits all" approach to instruction that can be standardized, measured, and assessed. Also contributing to the tension are competing notions about what the roles of teacher and student should look like. Luckily, Nueva School's ability to work as a community and utilize the new media literacy to create collective intelligence—*the ability to pool our knowledge toward a common goal*—helped them create solutions and results in a timely fashion, rather than falling into the mistakes of creating too many barriers or policies from the start or cutting conversation off at the knees before implementation even began.

As technology is introduced in schools, we need to be concerned about what is often referred to as the Participation Gap. Who in society has the knowledge and experience to meaningfully participate in these worlds we're talking about? Who feels empowered and entitled in this digital generation? How do we speak to those kids whose schools do not provide one laptop per child? Students who grow up in households that have access to Wikipedia, Facebook, and YouTube will have different experiences in the classroom from those who don't. Afterschool programs, library programs, and classroom programs have to help reduce that gap in participation. Such a divide could also easily unfold between teachers and students if schools don't offer teachers professional development and encourage them to play in the technology sandbox alongside their students.

Often, fear of the "new" stems from concern about failing. This is a mindset we need to change. We need to see our failures not as negatives, but as opportunities to learn and use them as ways to do better next time. As *Star Wars*' Jedi Master Yoda would say, "Train yourself to let go of everything you fear to lose." Luckily for you, *From Fear to Facebook* encourages schools to "learn by doing" as they build community, create systematic change, and become part of the movement where participatory learning becomes the norm instead of the exception.

Erin Reilly
Research Director, New Media Literacies

introduction

If you're not falling down every now and again,
it's a sign that you're not doing anything innovative.

−Woody Allen

I moved to California from central New Jersey in the summer of
2007. Buoyed by the "go west" optimism that has accompanied
many an American, I started my work as the assistant director and
head of the middle school at the Nueva School in Hillsborough,
California. Located just 20 minutes south of San Francisco along the
I-280 corridor, Nueva is home to a small private school community that includes many technologically sophisticated families from
Silicon Valley.

My experience of teaching history and serving as a department
chair and high school class dean for 14 years at Princeton Day School
in Princeton, New Jersey, made me confident that I could handle
the transition to my new leadership role at Nueva. As a classroom
teacher, I used technology and felt at ease with managing discussion forums with students, showing artwork and film clips on an
LCD projector, and maintaining regular e-mail communication
with students and parents. I relied on the help of more tech-savvy
colleagues to help me set up class conferences online and also to
navigate the LCD projector more skillfully. I was a competent technologist in the classroom.

When I arrived at Nueva, I fast learned that technology in central
New Jersey is not exactly the same as technology in Silicon Valley.
Innovation, risk-taking, bold planning and execution are the hall-
marks of daily life along the I-280 corridor. Also, the pace at which
technology moves in the Valley leaves the sleepy community of
Princeton in the dust. Nueva is located just miles from the tech

giants Apple, Google, Oracle, Yahoo, and Sun Microsystems, and the parent body is made up of many who work at these companies. Many of the children of these tech pioneers are students at Nueva.

One of the first projects handed to me was to launch the first year of the 1-to-1 laptop program at the school. I attempted to do my homework over the summer and reached out to schools that had already developed 1-to-1 programs. I was not sure about faculty readiness at Nueva, but my initial conversations with teachers revealed that they all felt confident about the move to a 1-to-1 program and were focusing much of their energy on the change away from laptop carts. Anyone who has lived through sharing carts can understand the frustration caused by having to share the machines, move the carts from classroom to classroom, recharge the batteries on the machines, and keep the wires from strangling each other.

The teachers' focus on getting rid of the laptop carts made perfect sense to me, since I had just come from a New Jersey school that also used them. Many of the teachers at Nueva already felt that the school was essentially a 1-to-1 school and that the transition to a 1-to-1 program would be smooth and without incident. I kept asking different people at school about the rollout, and everyone exuded confidence and reassurance.

Well, they could not have been more off base, and I could not have been more ill-prepared for the firestorm that would come my way as the leader of the 1-to-1 program at Nueva.

At the end of the first month of school, in my new role and in my new home state of California, I crouched in fear at what the school had wrought in giving a laptop to every student in Grades 6–8. My daily meetings with the head of the school started to feel a lot like conversations among people trapped in a bunker, as we attempted to troubleshoot security breaches, gaming, and home management of the laptops, and understand how the computers would affect classroom and school culture. We operated from a place of fear.

Students, teachers, and parents had different perspectives on the laptop situation, and we had to try to bring a community together around technology. Fractures appeared left and right, and one parent even suggested that we have a town hall–style meeting to air out parents' grievances and differences, which ranged from conflicts over whether students should be given unfettered access to the web—free of filters—to the belief of other parents that the entire program should be shut down then and there.

I was ready to pack my bags and head back to Jersey and the comforting voice of Bruce Springsteen, but I knew I could not walk away from this challenge, which offered me an opportunity to meet technology head-on. I had to take the leadership role, and I had to learn as much as I could as fast as possible. My self-image as a competent technologist from New Jersey was long gone.

This book is the story of my attempts to understand and embrace the changing landscape of technology in schools. As a school administrator and parent of two young children growing up as "digital natives," I feel strongly that schools need to educate students, teachers, and families about the perils and possibilities of technology.

My frame of reference has shifted and crystallized as I've become increasingly aware of the amazing potential technology has, not just to enhance, but to transform teaching and learning. I want my own children to benefit from this sea change taking place. The experience at Nueva underscores how important it is for schools to create technology laboratories for learning. Not a day passes when I do not see my own kids play with technology, whether it involves using a Flip Video camcorder to document my daughter learning how to ride a bicycle or my son helping my wife to complete her weekly newsletter in iWork's Pages program.

Schools cannot go it alone when they incorporate technology, and I learned that lesson the hard way in my experience launching the laptop program at Nueva. Ultimately, we ended up collaborating with many people and organizations in the course of establishing our 1-to-1 program. We reached out to organizations like Common Sense Media, a San Francisco–based national nonprofit organization committed to helping families with children live with media. We invited educator, technologist, and futurist Alan November to Nueva to run a professional development day for our teachers and then sent a team of teachers to his Building Learning Communities summer workshops. We consulted with Erin Reilly, research director of New Media Literacies, Los Angeles. We brought in cybersafety expert Steve DeWarns to speak to parents and students about smart online living. We organized a daylong boot-up camp at the start of the school year, in which we balanced a discussion of certain basic issues—physical care of the machines, school guidelines for computer usage, the safety and ethical issues that surround the use of computers—with media creation activities designed to show students the possibilities that technology offers. We held book discussions with parents, using Candace Kelsey's *Generation MySpace*. We surveyed our students and parents about media use at school and at home. We hosted parent evenings to discuss smart parenting strategies for healthy laptop living at home.

The key lesson we learned is that adults see technology as a source for information and a means of communication, while children view technology as a tool for entertainment and socializing. How can schools manage this cultural divide? Implementing a 1-to-1 laptop program brings this issue into sharper focus and forces communities to address the wide gulf between adults and children in the area of technology. Moving to a 1-to-1 program is not just about enhancing teaching and learning in an academic setting. It is about being open to the online world of students and being ready to deal with the social landscape that forms such an integral part of their lives.

The Nueva School motto is "Learn by Doing; Learn by Caring," and in our experiences with the 1-to-1 program, we tried to seize each situation as a learning opportunity, not only for ourselves, but also for the larger community. We framed a healthy, albeit difficult, ongoing conversation between school and home to bring the community closer together around technology.

A successful school program addresses and unites all three constituencies—students, teachers, and parents. Schools need to involve students directly in conversations about technology. Without student buy-in, a 1-to-1 laptop program is doomed to fail. Students are on the front lines of technology, and they need to feel included in the dialogue around appropriate use. Teachers need support and training to enter the multitasking world of their students. And, parents cannot survive the onslaught of a student laptop in the home unless they know how to create and sustain reasonable boundaries for its use after school hours.

Many parents freely admit they would like to remain in the Neolithic era with technology, and they are saddened to see children swept up in the technology tide. Schools need to help these parents respond with excitement instead of fear to the learning possibilities technology offers. Concerted parent education efforts are critical, coupled with communication with students about striking a balance between the desire for freedom and the need for boundaries in computer usage.

Nobody can tackle this protean challenge alone. Schools need to reach out to other schools, and parents need to know that they are not alone. Kids are the ones who are already connected everywhere.

The shift in thinking, from fear to Facebook (or opportunity), takes time for school communities to work through, and schools nationwide must steer a new course with technology right there to help navigate the sea change.

We can start by creating a carefully mapped technology infrastructure for schools. Through texting, e-mailing, blogging, and using Facebook and other current technologies, we can tap into the wealth of information available online, often in mere milliseconds, with an intelligently constructed electronic network engine. The current apparatus at use in schools is akin to the limited integration of America's utility system that Thomas Friedman describes in *Hot, Flat, and Crowded*. There are 3,200 electric utility companies in America, Friedman observes, and traversing the grid they have established is about as efficient as taking local roads only on a cross-country drive. In other words, just as the various utility companies must streamline their systems of communication and coverage, so, too, must the 14,000 U.S. school districts find a way to work together to arrive at a unified vision of 21st-century education.

In the words of one fellow educator: "We are standing at the cusp of a revolution in education." In a 2009 op-ed piece in the *New York Times*, Columbia University Professor Mark Taylor called for an "End [of] the University as We Know It," stating:

> For many years, I have told students, "Do not do what I do; rather, take whatever I have to offer and do with it what I could never imagine doing and then come back and tell me about it." My hope is that colleges and universities will be shaken out of their complacency and will open academia to a future we cannot conceive. (April 27, 2009)

This same thinking needs to trickle down to K–12 schools. The journey of the Nueva School and the rollout of its 1-to-1 laptop program provide an example to illustrate that now is the time for profound changes in the approach schools take with technology. The "future we cannot conceive" looks a lot like the present, and that is okay for schools to admit, but they also need to turn fear into innovation, meet kids where they are, educate parents and teachers, and head for the future with an entire community at their back.

chapter 1

lessons learned
Starting a 1-to-1 Laptop Program

Best-laid plans aren't necessarily successful plans!
Our ambitious 1-to-1 rollout didn't go as smoothly
as we'd hoped. Even with lessons learned, we found
more surprises and challenges in the second year.

In the 1983 film *War Games*, young David Lightman (played by Matthew Broderick) accidentally links into a top secret, national security–level computer simulation game designed to play out different war scenarios involving the United States and Russia. It all happens innocently enough. Bored in the afternoon after school, David has a friend over, Jennifer (played by Ally Sheedy), and the two of them playfully explore the potentialities of the game. They begin pressing buttons and giggle as different configurations pop up on the screen. Little do they know that they have mistakenly launched the countdown to World War III! On the other side of the computer screen, the national security team scrambles to figure out, in the words of one of them, "What the hell is going on?"

I began the school year at our opening faculty meeting in 2007 by showing a scene from this film. It fit perfectly with the launch of our 1-to-1 laptop program. I cautioned the faculty that we could very well end up looking like the national security team in the film, foolishly trying to keep up with the kids. Little did I know at that moment how clearly this film would resonate for all of us as we began to live out the 1-to-1 laptop program.

One of the primary reasons the school moved to a 1-to-1 laptop program was practical: to alleviate the logjam that had developed over the use of laptop carts. One teacher remembers the days of the laptop carts:

> It was a nightmare. There were two carts for the whole building. You had to sign up to use them. The wires were a mess. If you got them after 10:30 in the morning, the computers weren't charged, and there weren't enough outlets in the building to plug the machines in. And, more and more teachers were using the laptops, especially in Humanities. We couldn't stand it anymore. We had outgrown the existing technology, and we had to change for teaching and learning to keep moving forward. Each year, we were adding more laptops to the school inventory, and it finally made sense for all students to have their own laptops.

The situation was untenable for students as well. This same teacher explains: "The more students used the laptops in individual classes, the more frustrated they became when they learned that they had saved their work on different machines. It was an endless process to find their work."

In keeping with Nueva's philosophy and attitude toward risk-taking, the school took the bold step of implementing its laptop program in three grade levels, 6–8, at once, instead of beginning more cautiously with just one grade level and then rolling up or down. Interviews with graduating eighth graders at the end of the first year of the project indicated that this full-scale approach actually created some of the problems that manifested themselves throughout the first year. One eighth grade student wondered whether the fourth grade would be a better year to begin a laptop program: "It's before kids get into chatting and gaming, and they still listen to their parents and teachers." The idea of piloting the program with a few teachers and students prior to full delivery had not entered into our discussions.

Many of the teachers felt ill-prepared to deal with the problems that arose during the first year. However, as mentioned, before the rollout, few had expressed concern about the new program. In fact, I vividly recall one teacher stating, in a matter-of-fact manner, "We are already a 1-to-1 laptop school." In my conversations with those at other schools that use a vast laptop cart system, this was a similar refrain.

A tremendous amount of planning and thinking went into the decision to move to a 1-to-1 laptop program. For years, Nueva families had expressed frustration with the challenges of trying to traverse platforms, moving from a Mac to a PC, for example. Parents reported multiple instances in which their children had been unable to hand in assignments that they had completed at home because they could not print them at school. Problems arose for teachers in this regard as well when they found that students could not continue work on a project started in class unless they had the necessary software on their home machines. In addition, issues of economic equity arose, and the thinking was that the transition to a 1-to-1 laptop program would remove that issue, in that all students would have the same software package on their school-issued computers. For students with learning issues, such as dyslexia, the laptop program was a sure way to help them achieve greater academic success. One parent said flatly, "My child is dyslexic, and the 1-to-1 program will help him learn." Ultimately, though, the school wanted to create a smoother home–school connection with computers and remove the barriers to curricular innovation with technology.

Year One

The first year of the laptop program lived up to the school's motto of "Learn by Doing." The first day we distributed the computers, the students bubbled with excitement. We broke into small groups with our tech support staff and faculty to help students figure out passwords and mail accounts. In each room, keyboards clicked away, and the kids took off ... in directions we had not quite anticipated. They quickly discovered the iChat application and began videoconferencing and instant messaging. They started downloading games and building their iTunes libraries and even hacking the administrator password. It literally took only seconds for them to show all of us adults that when it comes to technology, we are light years behind this generation. As I walked from room to room, I was amazed at the electric feel among the students, but I was also struck by the deer-in-headlights look of the faculty. One faculty member asked, "Should we be worried about this? They are kind of going crazy with the laptops." Another faculty member stated, "*War Games* has begun!"

When we distributed the laptops to the students, our IT director made the point that the laptops were for the students to explore for programming and applications. She emphasized that if a student came across interesting software applications, the school would be open to deploying those applications. Our mistake was that we did not make it clear enough to the students that the laptops were school-owned machines, and we failed to punctuate that the purpose of the laptop program was to enhance teaching and learning in the academic environment. Therefore, the students were under the impression that the laptops were theirs to manipulate and configure in any way they saw fit. As a result, the students veered into areas we had not foreseen or understood.

In Samuel Freedman's *New York Times* article, "New Class(room) War: Teacher vs. Technology," Professor Michael Bugeja, director of the journalism school at Iowa State University, is quoted: "The baby boomers seem to see technology as information and communication. Their offspring and the emerging generation seem to see the same devices as entertainment and socializing" (November 7, 2007). At Nueva, teachers wanted to explore applications with students and develop online courses, but the students' focus was on the social possibilities that the laptops brought. There was a profound disconnect between teachers and students, and we realized that we needed to find ways to bridge the gap.

One teacher jumped right into the fray and tackled many of the issues that accompanied the laptops. Her view is that teachers need to multitask in the classroom to "meet the students where they are." She moved her entire science class online: students use electronic lab notebooks and submit assignments online, and she designs dynamic electronic presentations that make use of the best of YouTube, Google Images, and music. Because she has two teenage children of her own, she has already experienced the challenge of parenting in the age of technology, and she knows where these middle school students are headed. But it still takes a certain fearlessness to approach teaching this way. She is not afraid to fail; she routinely seeks input from the students on how to use applications and how to maximize learning with technology. Not every teacher is as comfortable with the computers. When this teacher shared her techniques and strategies in a presentation at a staff meeting, many of her colleagues stared in awe at all that she does. However, one faculty member stated, "It's great that you are doing all of that, but there is no way I can do that. I'll stick to paper and books."

Even teachers who admit to being technology novices recognize that curriculum needs to meet the students in this area. In a unit on expository writing, one such teacher decided to use a mock trial simulation to facilitate the use of technology and dialogue around the issue of cyberstalking. The topic was timely, given the tragic suicide of Megan Meier, the 13-year-old girl who fell prey to an appalling hoax on MySpace.

Megan's story acted as a backdrop to the trial. One of the written assessments asked students to compare her story to that of the victim in the cyberstalking mock trial. This activity captivated the students, and they soared with a deep, meaningful learning experience and authentic uses of technology. Each legal team created a blog to share legal strategy, and students posted late into the night. Jury members took careful notes on their laptops during trial proceedings. Using the video camera on the laptop, students recorded the opening and closing statements and assessed the "lawyers'" performances. Instead of serving as a distraction, in this situation the laptops enhanced teaching and learning. Where earlier in the semester this teacher had battled students over appropriate use in the classroom and staying on task when writing, she now had success in harnessing their collective energy around an authentic learning experience.

Another teacher attempted to engage in the laptop debate with students and used the opportunity to teach expository writing. He had the students watch excerpts of the PBS *Frontline* episode "Growing Up Online" (www.pbs.org/wgbh/pages/frontline/kidsonline/), and then asked them to take stands on privacy and safety issues. The class erupted so passionately that he could not appropriately direct their energy. He quickly abandoned the project and let me know that he "wished me luck" in handling the student outcry. He simply did not want to get caught in the crossfire of negotiating privacy and safety with free use and fair use issues for students.

At Kansas State University, in an Introduction to Cultural Anthropology course, 200 students began a brainstorming exercise to think about how students learn. With the use of Google Documents, these students quickly gathered input and created a short video, *A Vision of Students Today* (www.youtube.com/watch?v=dGCJ46vyR9o). The video underscores the outdated nature of teaching and learning today and offers a wonderful glimpse into the minds of the current generation of students. The camera flashes across the lecture hall and finds students holding up placards with different tidbits of information about their technology usage over the course of a year, from the number of pages of e-mails read (500), to the number of Facebook profiles read (1,281), to the number of web pages read (2,300). The point: these students learn differently from those of the past, and pedagogy needs to keep pace.

One response to this situation is simply to draw battle lines, as does Professor Ali Nazemi of Roanoke College, as quoted in Freedman's "New Class(room) War: Teacher vs. Technology" in the *New York Times*:

> If you start tolerating this stuff [students' inappropriate use of technology], it becomes the norm. The more you give, the more they take. These devices become an indispensable sort of thing for the students. And nothing should be indispensable. Multitasking is good, but I want them to do more tasking in class. (November 7, 2007)

I admire Professor Nazemi's resolve, but as Freedman goes on to say, "Too bad the good guy is going to lose."

At Nueva, we discovered firsthand that the good guy might lose. In the early part of the first year, we were losing the laptop battle and losing badly. In the first few weeks, students routinely sent instant messages to their peers while in class. In the middle of one class, a student instant-messaged his mother to find out what was for dinner that night. Video chatting with iChat was rampant after school, and during one chat session, a student even shared a view of his mother in her pajamas. Many parents grew increasingly alarmed and did not know how to engage their children in conversation about appropriate computer use at home. For their part, teachers felt overwhelmed by the task of managing the distractions in their classrooms, and one faculty member announced, "I won't use the laptops in my classroom. The kids need to be able to focus."

It became more and more apparent that we had an epidemic on our hands. The community had broken into two camps: on one side stood faculty and parents who felt that students needed the freedom to explore and learn with little or no restriction; on the other side, parents dug their heels in over the need for more restrictions on laptop use, both at school and at home. At informal "parent coffees," these issues boiled to the surface and erupted into heated disagreements over the appropriate direction the school should take. One parent suggested holding a town meeting to allow students and parents the opportunity to hash it out in a free-for-all atmosphere. Some parents felt blindsided by the laptops. They had created carefully considered home guidelines for the use of instant messaging, and their children now came home with school-issued machines that granted permission to video chat with their peers. The school, in their minds, had made a decision for the home, and they had been given no choice in the matter. Still other parents saw this whole experience as a wonderful opportunity to engage the students and to educate them on appropriate use.

The school had to make a decision. To the dismay of many, we blocked iChat on the school laptops. Little did I know that the outcry would be so severe and extreme. I received volumes of correspondence on both sides of the issue. Student council speeches sounded the clarion call for retraction. Students put together petitions to protest. One student wrote,

> We really love it [iChat] and use it for important uses. We think that one reason is the parents. We believe that the parents can block it for their own children if they want, but it is not fair for them to block it for the whole middle school. If they do not know how, they can ask tech help for help on blocking it for their individual child.

Other students were less circumspect, however:

> My mom says that the majority of angry old people are okay with video chat at school, however after 3:30 it should go off. Of course this makes sense that instead of doing as they say, you ban iChat overall. Pretty smart. Fair enough, it was too complex to turn it off at a certain

time. A lot easier. I am actually glad that you decided on a blanket ban. Otherwise it would be like teasing us. Giving it to us for a little bit then taking it away. Boy, that would be horrible!

One teacher commented, "At least they have a cause now for their student council speeches. This is the most interesting election in years."

Many parents also sharpened their quills and shared their opinions on the chat issue. One parent wrote:

> iChat was wonderful. It truly broke the clique boundaries that tend to occur at school. Also as our daughter is very busy, and goes to a commuter school, she has almost no social life. We, as parents, were relieved that the clique boundary seemed broken on iChat and that she was engaging socially with her classmates. I also second the opinion expressed by other parents, that iChat is like TV or video games or Internet browsing. It is the responsibility of the parent to teach the children how best to use these tools. Each parent can establish household rules as they wish. We are in favor of bringing iChat back! Censorship is not necessary, nor wanted.

The situation had turned into a first amendment issue of freedom of speech. The parent just quoted takes responsibility for her daughter and is willing to attempt to set boundaries at home, and she was pleased that the application offered her daughter a new social outlet. Of this there was never any doubt, but from the school's perspective, the academic purpose of the laptops had disappeared into the vortex of social networking, especially when it was occurring during the school day.

Another parent saw the iChat storm of protest as a "tempest in a teapot." She stated:

> We will monitor her use, set limits, and help her learn to manage her time efficiently. I think once the novelty wears

off and children realize how much work they have to do, they will naturally reduce their use of the tool. Parents and school staff can help children learn good time management skills more effectively by "learning by doing" as opposed to the school making the decision for the children.

Viewed as a top-down decision, our approach brought the relationship between home and school to the surface and called into question the boundary issues associated with the two realms.

Other parents were grateful that the school took the approach it did. One of them commented:

> Thank you for blocking iChat. You acted with due diligence. We felt betrayed by the school when our child came home with the application and started instant messaging, when we had not yet entered that realm in our household. When we told her that we didn't want her instant messaging, she responded with, "But mom, the school gave us this laptop with iChat!" Now that you have blocked its use, we feel better able to enter this area at our own pace, instead of being forced into it by the school.

Respect for the ability of parents to make these decisions in their own homes factored into our decision to block the use of iChat. And, particularly with middle school students, the option of allowing some to use iChat after school, on a case-by-case, family-by-family decision, did not present itself as a viable alternative. We did not want to aggravate an already frustrated community and pit those who had access against those who did not.

Our next task centered on parent education. We offered to hold a book discussion on *Generation MySpace*, written by Candice Kelsey, an educator who has spent years dealing and negotiating with the online dramas of social networking among her students. This book is an excellent resource and offers practical advice to parents and teachers. Kelsey frames how to have the conversation about appropriate computer use and even gives sample dialogues to have with children. During the book discussion, I had an aha! moment that helped me better understand why the iChat situation had caused such uproar. As parents shared their stories about trying to understand the home-computing environment with their children, it became clear that the parents were starting to clue in to the online activity of their children. This thought is terrifying to middle school students. Finally, the adults were starting to get their heads out of the sand. For the students, the days of unmonitored surfing, chatting, and blogging were coming to an end.

One parent shared, "My daughter, who is in high school, just got her Facebook account, but she assured me that it is secure and can only be used for school." The room fell silent. She could sense that she had missed something.

 What is Facebook, and who has access to Facebook profiles?

Facebook is a free social networking site—in 2009 it took the lead as the most used social networking site in the world, well ahead of MySpace and Twitter (http://blog.compete.com/2009/02/09/facebook-myspace-twitter-social-network/). According to the Facebook user agreement, users are required to be age 13 and older. Users can create settings on their Facebook profiles to limit public access to their profiles, or they can have their Facebook profiles open to the public. Many users choose to create settings so that only their friends have access to photos and personal information. Users new to Facebook sometimes set themselves up to unintended public exposure by not creating stringent enough privacy settings or providing too much personal information.

What should parents know about Facebook? A good starting point is the website Facebook for Parents (www.facebookforparents.org).

"What?" she asked. We then filled her in on how Facebook works and who might have access to her daughter's page. She replied, "My God, I had no idea. I need to have a conversation with her about this." She then did have the conversation with her, and she now routinely checks her daughter's Facebook profile. I can only imagine how disappointed her daughter is.

To help parents gain firm footing at home, we decided to offer content barrier software to families. We purchased a license for ContentBarrier, a content-filtering program, for each child in the middle school. By default, the program is quite restrictive, which prevented us from deploying it automatically to all computers. The decision to permit or block content is a personal one each family must make for itself. In addition, we invited Officer Steve DeWarns, who has dedicated himself to online child exploitation cases and to educating the public about online safety, to speak to our students. He has appeared on *The Today Show* and *Dr. Phil*, in addition to giving presentations to hundreds of schools in California. Officer DeWarns discussed the disclosure of personal information online, in chat rooms, gaming, and during instant messaging and offered caveats that accompany all of these forms of communication. One parent shared the response at home to his talk:

> This seemed to really resonate with the kids. We had been trying to convey some of the points these girls learned today for awhile, but couldn't seem to get buy-in. The example of the girl trying to pull the photo off the bulletin board was really powerful and a great visual aid to illustrate how "public and forever" all their photos/e-mails are once they post this stuff on the Internet. It's a hard, abstract concept for the kids to grasp, but I think the officer finally got the point across to these girls. Lord knows we have been trying!

The Ad Council has developed several wonderful short ads to facilitate such conversations and to help students further see the difference in challenges encountered by online personas as opposed to those that occur with face-to-face contact. One powerful ad shows a female middle school student walking through various parts of her community with adults and fellow teens commenting on her postings. Three adult males comment on the young woman's tattoos and underwear and ask, "Sarah, when are you going to post something new?" The young girl's facial expression sours as she realizes that she has revealed too much of herself online.

Another ad underscores the power that unkind words can have online by showing four teenage girls seated around a kitchen table, then zooming in on one girl uttering outrageously hurtful words—"tramp, zitface, clown, ugly"—to one of her friends. The ad finishes with the question, "If you wouldn't say it in person, why say it online?" Taking time with students to talk through such challenges opens an important dialogue and signals that the adults are listening. When an online transgression takes place, students know that they can reach out to an adult in their life to help them figure out how to confront or deal with cyberissues.

When other problems arise, such as gaming or e-mailing in class, we deal with the situation on a case-by-case basis. The teacher confronts the student, addresses the problem, and then writes a brief note home, requesting the parents have a conversation with their child. Parents are then asked to report back to the teacher on the content of the discussion. This approach has generated a healthy dialogue between school and home. For more serious matters, such as hacking the administrator password, we reimage the student's computer so that it is returned to the initial configurations. iTunes libraries and other downloads are wiped clean, but document files are preserved. These consequences are effective, and the conversations that arise from these situations elevate the importance of integrity for responsible use.

However, the issue of buy-in weighs heavily, especially when it comes to instituting an acceptable use policy (AUP). At Nueva, we did not adequately create a sense of ownership of the AUP, and the students revolted—they refused to sign Nueva's acceptable use policy. When, at the end of the first week of the program, the school sent a letter home detailing the parameters of the AUP and requesting adherence to it through a signature, only 7 of 120 were signed. The school did not get overwhelming support from the families on this issue: in fact, many parents were proud that their children had refused to accept the AUP on the basis of principle. This was surprising since Nueva parents, in order to receive access to Nueva's website, had willingly signed a document that is the equivalent of the federal tax code, with almost every detail of online life enumerated.

We did not require students to sign the AUP from the start, nor did we establish buy-in with students. Therefore, at the end of the year, we only had 63 of 120 AUPs on file. When I shared this information with educators at other schools, they all looked at me with incredulity and even admiration. One educator remarked: "Your students actually read about and care about the AUP? That's actually a good problem to have." We took the long view on the AUP issue and chose to work to educate parents, teachers, and students on proper use.

It is never easy to figure out a way to go over rules for proper computer use with middle school students. To arrive at a workable plan to live cooperatively with technology in a school community, a fine line must be straddled between paternal guidance and student voices. Making a real-world connection with students and parents helps provide context for the "why" of an acceptable use policy. By year three, we had figured out how to enter this conversation with students, and, in so doing, we referred to several real-world situations.

For example, the U.S. military found itself trapped in the crosshairs as it tried to leverage technology for advancement and progress, while figuring out how to shield and safeguard the precious vault of information that undergirds its organization.

The military is toying with an extreme technology makeover, harnessing the tools of Facebook, Twitter, YouTube, and Flickr to overhaul its image to bring in recruits and influence public opinion. However, the military is expected to unfurl a new policy to limit the uses of social networking, owing to increased worries about cybersecurity. This may thwart whatever progress has been made and sink popular blogs, such as Embrace the Suck, which chronicles life at the front in Afghanistan. The debate, James Dao of the *New York Times* writes, "reflects a broader clash of cultures; between the anarchic, unfiltered, bottom-up nature of the web and the hierarchical, tightly controlled top-down tradition of the military" ("Pentagon Keeps Wary Watch as Troops Blog," September 8, 2009).

Funnily enough, this is just what our students said about school authorities trying to implement an AUP for school computers.

Another organization, the National Football League, banned the use of Twitter during training camp, for fear that players would leak team secrets and playbooks. The notorious hothead and Bengals wide receiver Chad Ochocinco (formerly Johnson) responded to this, of course, on his Twitter page: "Damn NFL and these rules, I am going by my own set of rules" (@OGOchoCinco).

Even lawyers are being hushed, as bar associations put the clamps on those who use blogs to spread news about courtroom happenings. John Schwartz of the *New York Times* reported the fining of a Florida lawyer, Sean Conway, who called a judge an "Evil, Unfair Witch" in a blog. With more and more twenty-somethings entering the legal profession, the problem of inappropriate postings will only worsen, according to Stephen Gillers of New York University Law School. In the same *Times* article, Gillers says, "Twenty-somethings have a much-reduced sense of personal privacy" ("A Legal Battle: Online Attitude vs. Rules of the Bar," September 12, 2009).

Students want to have control over their computers at school. They want to download and personalize their music libraries, chat with their peers using iChat, clog school bandwidth with YouTube videos, and bypass any effort to regulate network security, all in the name of technology independence. Schools have an obligation to provide safe learning environments, but they also are charged with fostering innovation and creativity.

The question is, "How wide should the window of use be opened to enhance teaching and learning?" There is simply no way to stop the flow of information, as Noah Shachtman, editor of *Wired*'s national security blog, Danger Room, commented in Dao's *New York Times* article about the military (September 8, 2009). Schools are in the same pickle. Schools must help students to make sense of information, to synthesize, analyze, and judge the credibility of the material they encounter.

But schools also need to draw boundaries for students around issues like chatting, texting, downloading, and gaming, much to the chagrin of freewheeling students, many of whom are accustomed to more lax rules at home surrounding technology.

Is there a way to find a win–win solution? One way is to invite students into the conversation about setting boundaries for proper use in school. This is a tricky process and one that can fast spin into open revolt, as we learned in the first year of the laptop program at Nueva.

Schools can devise laptop boot-up days to introduce students to both the perils and possibilities of technology. These boot-ups can include workshops on care, ethics, and appropriate use guidelines, but they should also give time and attention to authentic media creation projects and experiences so that students, with the guidance of teachers, can experiment with the tools, make mistakes and missteps, and learn. Also, schools can invite guest speakers in the field of technology to share success stories of innovation and risk-taking. Technology educators can also be brought in to run aspects of the boot-up camp to bring outside voices into the community dialogue.

An additional, critical component of the rollout of computer use in schools is to engage the parent community. Parents are spokes on the wheel of the school community, and for the educational ride to go smoothly, schools need to educate parents about appropriate use at home, particularly when it comes to such tools as Facebook, MySpace, Twitter, and Flickr. Students will receive mixed messages if, after a night of unfettered computer use at home, they come to school to find a more restrictive policy in place, and this is where conflict arises. Organizations such as Common Sense Media, a national nonprofit organization based in San Francisco, have created a family media use agreement that schools and families can use together to arrive at agreements for appropriate use. Bringing families to school to talk with administrators and teachers about these issues helps bridge the gap that can exist between children and adults around technology.

In terms of the actual policies that schools implement, schools need to provide wiggle room in them so that the policies can be modified and adapted according to circumstances that arise during the school day. Having an AUP in a question and answer (Q and A) format leaves room for new questions to be added as issues unfold. Not every situation can be addressed in an AUP, and it is critical that the document conveys a spirit of encouraging students to do the right thing. The last thing schools should do is box themselves into a corner with a document that interferes with the ability of teachers to help students act appropriately with technology. We figured this out in year three when we moved to a Q and A format for our acceptable use policy. By the second week of school, when we handed out the laptops to students after the boot-up day and with the new Q and A format, we had 100% acceptance of our AUP and no grumbling.

AUPs can be a challenge for teachers. Some teachers become so wedded to enforcing the "letter of the law" that they lose the ability to act in the moment and educate students. One teacher, running a study hall, grew worried that students were playing games and not doing homework on their laptops. He sent me an e-mail during the study hall and asked me to contact the tech office to use Apple Remote Desktop to survey student activity in the study hall. The result: students were actually doing their homework and not playing games, as he had suspected. This teacher felt unable to deal with the students in the study hall because the AUP did not specifically mention the use of computers during study hall. Schools cannot reach the point where teachers need to walk around with the AUP in their pocket, pull it out, and then point to code, paragraph, and line to call students on their behavior. Instead, schools need to foster a spirit of discussion and reflection and impose appropriate consequences when there are clear transgressions.

During year one, a wonderful learning opportunity to educate fifth grade students about acceptable use, a year in advance of their entry into the 1-to-1 laptop program, arose around the use of Gmail at school. Several students opened Gmail accounts, and many did so without the permission of their parents. While we do not have a 1-to-1 laptop program at the fifth grade level, the students take a tech class, and humanities and math teachers use a laptop cart for projects. Also, students have computer access in the library at recess and lunch. In a matter of days, these students began using the chat function in Gmail during classes, and word of this traveled quickly among the grade. I began to receive e-mails from students who were concerned about the rampant use. One student wrote:

> I have been noticing a lot of people Gmail chatting during classes. I keep telling them to stop but they will not. When I try to get them to stop they start calling me a baby for not chatting during class. They get mad whenever I tell them that we should be trying to learn in class not chat they just ignore me.

I shared his comments with the fifth grade teaching team, and they addressed the use of Gmail at school with the students.

Concurrently with this student's e-mail to me, parents raised the issue of Gmail use at school at a morning coffee gathering, and I explained to them that we have several safeguards in place to monitor computer use. One of these safeguards is Apple Remote Desktop, which allows the school to access computer screens on campus. After the coffee, one parent went home and asked his daughter if she had a Gmail account. The fifth grader confessed that she did have the account, and the father shared with her the content of my discussion with parents concerning the issue. He also disclosed to her that the school uses Apple Remote Desktop to monitor student use. This student then sent an instant message to all of her peers, alerting them that the parents and the school had discovered the "surreptitious" use of Gmail and that there would soon be "big trouble."

The next day in class, discussion erupted over privacy issues and concern that the school had too much power. However, as conversation continued, under the guidance of a skillful Social and Emotional Learning (SEL) teacher, students began to arrive at the conclusion that the use of Gmail at school was not okay. They formed an agreement to cease using their accounts during school, and by the end of that day, two students came to my office to let me know that they had been using Gmail at school and were now going to stop. In addition, the student who had sent me the e-mail the night before came to see me. He was worried that his friends were going to get into "big trouble" for using Gmail. I reassured him that nobody was in trouble and that I appreciated his courage in coming forward to raise the issue with me. I thanked him for his leadership and let him know that he had set in motion a community conversation around appropriate use of e-mail at school. He responded, "It's good that we are having this discussion now before we get those laptops!" In a 24-hour period, we had made huge inroads with these 10-year-olds who were months away from receiving school laptops.

At the end of year one, we implemented several steps designed to help prepare students, parents, and teachers for the 1-to-1 laptop program. These included the following:

- A boot-up camp at the opening of school for our sixth graders to orient them to the laptops
- A partnership with Common Sense Media, an organization geared toward helping kids and families make informed choices about media

- Training sessions on how to conduct effective, efficient online research

- Faculty training and teacher-led technology workshops throughout the school year

- Parent education workshops to help navigate usage of the laptops between home and school

- Requiring a signed AUP before laptop distribution

- A programming elective offered to seventh and eighth grade students (to redirect the energy of the hackers who bypassed administrator security)

- Continued flexibility and openness in our approach to handling issues that arise

Year Two

Of course, the best-laid plans always bring surprises. At the start of year two, we created a carefully mapped-out week of boot-up camp for the students. This included faculty-led workshops on ethical dilemmas, a review of the acceptable use policy (AUP), with a quiz to discuss "gray" areas, an introduction to the menu of applications on the laptops, and detailed demonstrations of appropriate laptop care strategies. In addition, Common Sense Media ran two workshops for parents on how to develop home guidelines for computer usage with their children. Officer Steve DeWarns also spoke with students and parents about cyberbullying and online safety. The boot-up camp week appeared to roll out the laptops without incident. At the technology committee meeting toward the end of the week, after the completion of these various components of the boot-up program, we congratulated ourselves for "getting it right" with students. In fact, one member of the committee stated, "This could not have gone better."

At the conclusion of the all-school assembly on the Friday of the boot-up camp week, at 1:59 and 42 seconds p.m. (the time is forever etched into my memory), the wheels came off, and another communitywide crisis enveloped us. The faculty member running the assembly handed the microphone to an eighth grade student who wished to speak. He walked over to me and asked, "Did you plan this?" I responded with incredulity, "Ah, no." The head of school, who was standing right next to me, asked, "What do you think she is going to do?"

Before I could reply, the student asked, in a fire-and-brimstone voice, "How many students here agree with the terms of the acceptable use policy?" One very brave student raised his hand. Then, she turned the question: "How many students here disagree with the AUP?" A loud roar erupted and every other student joined her in a chant of "Down with the AUP! Down with the AUP!" The head of school looked at me in bewilderment and uttered, "Oh, dear." Students then filed out of the assembly, high-fiving each other and brimming with excitement at the public protest.

That Sunday afternoon, I received a phone call from the student who had spoken at the assembly, demanding that I participate in a conference call with the entire middle school community. I declined and assured her that we would have a community meeting the next day to discuss the acceptable use policy. With the head of school and another teacher, we developed a plan for the meeting. Students would fill out a note card and identify three parts of the AUP with which they disagreed. We would then have lunch meetings through the week with small groups of students to discuss the issues, which centered on being able to use the laptops on school buses, to and from school, at lunch, recess, and in after-school (After Care) classes to do homework.

The meeting started smoothly. I acknowledged the eighth grade student's protest from the previous Friday and framed her words in the historical context of the power of protest, from the civil rights movement and the student-led campus protests of the 1960s. I even quoted the words of Frederick Douglass, the legendary 19th-century civil rights activist: "If there is no struggle, there is no progress." I explained the approach we were going to use to work through the disagreements, had the students fill out the note cards, and then announced that students would go to meet in advisory groups to process the laptop issues. All appeared calm, at last.

As I stepped away from the microphone, however, the eighth grade student leader stood up with a prepared speech and announced to the entire group, "In direct disobedience of Matt [the middle school head] and Diane [the executive director of Nueva], I must be heard!" She proceeded to recite her demands, which centered on the overarching theme of building trust in a community and the practical concerns of being able to do homework on the bus. She also took issue with the fact that students had not been involved in creating the school's acceptable use policy. She was not wrong; this is where we had erred.

We constructed the AUP as a faculty, but we omitted a certain key constituency, the students. At the end of year one, in a meeting to debrief and review year one of the laptop program, we worked our way through the many issues we had experienced with students. Some teachers went so far as to move to eliminate the program entirely and yearned to return to simpler days of the laptop carts. The focus of the discussion with teachers centered on their feeling that the laptops had dismantled and derailed a strong school culture that emphasized play, trust, and cooperation. There was universal agreement that students needed to be brought back into the fold of the school's culture and that one key way to do this was to eliminate the use of the laptops at recess to encourage students to play outside and socialize with friends.

Another important area of contention dealt with monitoring in the classroom and the need to create and communicate the expectation that the laptops were to be used primarily for school-related learning. In the first year of the program, students had been allowed to veer into territories beyond school work, such as gaming and social networking, in their computer usage. However, as one faculty member stated quite clearly, the key problem was that students and adults had different views of the role of technology to enhance learning:

> For students, play and work are the same thing with technology. They are completely interwoven for them. For us, we make a division between work on the computer and our personal and social lives. We need to come to terms with that to make this program run smoothly.

Other parts of the discussion with teachers addressed the practical matters of getting rid of the technical hurdles that inhibited smooth running of the laptops during class time, such as printer issues and the ability of students to access the school server from home. Also, teachers wanted to make sure that students were required to and versed in putting their homework in a "drop box" on the server for each of their subjects, to facilitate development of an online portfolio. We combed through these many issues and felt confident that we had hit on the key points to include in the revised acceptable use policy. But we soon realized that we were looking at the AUP from the outside in and not from the inside out—from the student's point of view.

In my opening words to the students at the community meeting, I tried to spell out the need for the school to balance safety with freedoms, but clearly my words did not make much of an impact. Several teachers lauded this student for her courage in speaking up, and those teachers who had witnessed this student's growth over several years at the school marveled at her poise, confidence, and command in speaking in front of the entire community. One of these teachers said, "She would never have done this four years ago. We are so proud of her."

The student leader channeled her energies into a run for student council president. Her campaign speech, though still tempered, captured a wonderful sentiment for school communities to foster in its students:

When I stood up at assembly two weeks ago, I did so firstly for myself. I was fed up. When I spoke at MS [Nueva Middle School] Meeting, I did so not only for myself but for others. I will speak, in the future, for you. The Student Council's purpose is to represent the students to the teachers—to act as a go-between, a force of communication. May it do so this year—represent the students, represent their needs and wants, their problems. May it act as a voice of reason, to mediate communications between the faculty and students. May it create opportunities, and may it create a stronger community in the Nueva Middle School. May it have power, but not control it. May it be a voice for those who cannot shout above the crowd. I cannot promise you that I will succeed. I cannot promise change, and I cannot promise stability. I cannot even promise a fourth dance and popcorn. The only thing I can promise is that I will try, and that I will try with all my strength, to listen to you, to speak for you, to speak with you. I will speak your views, even should they not be mine, and I will do my best to create a lasting culture at Nueva—one of community and of honesty.

At parent coffees, held right in the midst of the AUP turmoil, parents celebrated the student's boldness and appreciated that the school was listening to the demands. One parent commented:

We think it's great that you [the school] are allowing the students to voice their concerns, but don't change any of the rules. We support you completely, but we just don't want to have to do this at home. It's better if you guys stay strict.

Another parent, in alignment with her child's stance in opposition to the AUP, wrote:

He has informed us that he has strong objections to portions of the acceptable use policy for school laptops, and that because of this he is unwilling to sign the form. We have decided to support him in taking this position on the condition that he engages in a respectful and constructive dialogue with you and others involved in administering the laptop program regarding the possibility of modifying parts of the AUP. He is working with some other students to draft a revised AUP to discuss with you. We hope that this situation will be seen as a positive development, since an implicit part of Nueva's mission is to educate future leaders capable of thinking for themselves, and it is probably a measure of the school's success that its students are taking action on something that they feel strongly about.

I shared our challenges with a head from another school to seek advice on how to handle the maelstrom. She chuckled and said:

You've got some little protesters over there at Nueva. This honestly would not happen at our school. Our students are not wired that way.

She did agree with the process we were using and thought a resolution was imminent. Her advice:

Give the students something, but not everything. You need to keep school running smoothly and provide a safe learning environment. Some issues you cannot bend on, like the bus, which is a matter of safety.

Teachers began to look for alternatives to meet the students halfway and realized that the students' concerns focused on practical matters such as completing homework. One faculty member proposed a solution:

It seems to me that without conceding anything in the AUP, we could give students what they really want, which is more opportunities to use their computers at school besides in class. I'd be willing to supervise laptop use one recess a week.

The lunch meetings were well attended by students, and one student proudly announced as he walked into one of the meetings, "It's time for me to help my community!" Students shared concerns about homework completion and computer use on buses, after school, and at recess. They listened to each other and felt honored to be part of the process of finding a solution for the school.

The eighth grade student leader even shifted in her thinking:

> I'm glad we're all working together and realize that we're all working for the same goals. I realize that we can't change everything, and that some things have already been irrevocably set for this year, but hope that maybe things can be different next year. I know some things are in there because of student misbehavior last year, and I hope that we can help the student body to understand the importance of their decisions about laptop care instead of merely dishing out constraints.

As a concession to students and in an attempt to listen to their concerns and implement change based on these concerns, we allowed laptop use during recess three days a week, with the proviso that students had to work on homework while in the laptop recess room. Ironically, once we put this in place, very few students showed up to use their laptops at recess. Instead, they played outdoors as we had hoped they would do.

Tim Brown, the CEO of IDEO, a design and innovation consultancy firm based in Palo Alto, California, in an October 9, 2009, interview with National Public Radio about IDEO's involvement in health care reform, explains the challenges that change can pose for a community:

> [W]hen something's designed on the outside and then pushed into the organization, there's often a lot of resistance. But when you involve the people themselves, then they already own the new solution, and it's so much easier then to get the change to happen.

We learned this valuable lesson from the students at Nueva.

For schools to be successful with rolling out a 1-to-1 laptop program, students need to be brought into the development and deployment of the program, from soup to nuts. The rules or guidelines need to be constructed with their input and also allow room for change over time. Tim Brown, in a September 23, 2009, interview with BNET, echoes this sentiment:

> It has to be an experimental culture. There has to be an enthusiasm for new ideas. You have to have a culture that's willing to explore new ideas, test them and then get rid of them if they're not good ideas. If ideas get shut down, if they're only allowed to happen in some little corner, or if only certain people are allowed to have ideas, then you're failing to tap into the innovation potential of an organization. So this notion of experimentation is thoroughly important.

At Nueva, we attempt to foster this culture of experimentation.

The school has a formal partnership with Stanford's design school and is in the process of developing a comprehensive design thinking curriculum for K–12 schools. In 2007, Nueva opened the doors of its Innovation Lab (iLab) and each day brings students into the lab for class projects. These projects range from figuring out how to lower an egg from the second floor of a building using a deck of cards and stapler, to constructing an optimally efficient solar house with the aid of a laser cutter, Adobe Illustrator, math, science, and design thinking. In his June 2008 *Harvard Business Review* article, Tim Brown defines design thinking "as a discipline that uses the designer's sensibility and methods to match people's needs with what is technologically feasible." Even though we did not know it at the time, Brown's definition captures perfectly what Nueva worked through in unfolding its 1-to-1 laptop program.

The rationale for a 1-to-1 laptop program needs to be clearly spelled out, and students, teachers, and parents need to be given adequate time to digest it. In addition, the home–school connection needs to be strong so that parents and school can work together to reinforce a consistent message to students. In a conversation I had with our IT director, who spearheaded the first year of the program, she underscored this point for schools:

> In year zero, there needs to be massive parent education. They need to know how to manage the home computing environment. All of the stuff they saw in their homes as a result of the computers coming home from school was already going on. They just did not know it. Also, teachers need heavy-duty training, curricular leadership, and rethinking about how to change their teaching to incorporate technology. There was a feeling among teachers that because the school had laptop carts and teachers used them in the classroom, the 1-to-1 program would be a natural extension. This turned out not to be the case.

There were moments when we asked ourselves why we had ever embarked on this program. However, we seized each new situation and moment as a learning opportunity, not only for ourselves but also for the community at large. Moving to a 1-to-1 program is not just about enhancing teaching and learning in an academic setting. It is about being open to the online world of students and being ready to deal with the social landscape that forms such an integral part of their lives.

chapter 2

schools and facebook

Moving Too Fast, or Not Fast Enough?

> Middle school students are social; thus, it is no surprise that they view technology as a social tool. We strove to find a working balance between the needs and work styles of students and the security and learning needs of the school.

When I purchased my iPhone, I braced myself for the four-hour online tutorial to learn how to navigate the device. However, just as I was sitting down to begin the tutorial, my 8-year-old son told me not to waste my time. He could teach me to use the phone in 20 minutes, he stated boldly. All he needed was a little time to "play" with it. Sure enough, he proved to be a better and more entertaining teacher than the online tutorial, and I quickly learned the basics of iPhone use. He continues to be my iPhone navigator, updating the phone, looking for "cool" applications, or apps, to add, and explaining the phone to me in clear, easy to understand language. Technology has flipped our roles. It used to be that parents and teachers taught children. Now, the reverse is also true, and the quicker we can grasp this concept, the better equipped we will all be to live in the 21st century.

Schools need to embrace this mindset. Students are quickly growing disenchanted with the snail's pace of change going on in classrooms regarding teaching with technology. Thankfully, some teachers have grabbed the mantle and are taking steps to meet students where they are in the online world. One talented tenth grade history teacher, a former colleague of mine at Princeton Day School, cooked up an entire 20th-century China project on Facebook. Students adopted the personalities of Sun Yat-sen, Mao Zedong, and Chang Kai-shek and created and updated Facebook pages and profiles for them, replete with photos and wall postings. In the words of the teacher: "This project changed the classroom. Students were so motivated and put far more hours into their research than they would have done with a traditional project."

The best part about this project was the organic way it developed in the hands of a teacher who listens to her students. As the class brainstormed the beginning stages of the unit, one of the students simply suggested that the class create Facebook pages for the three leaders and be required to chat, post, and debate online. Instead of balking at this potentially outlandish idea, this teacher jumped at the opportunity. This is exactly the kind of collaborative learning that the 21st century demands, but it does mean surrendering a bit of curricular control to the students. For many teachers, letting students "run" the show poses a challenge to the traditional "sage on the stage" model, even in the most progressive of teaching environments. The time has come to share the reins with students.

A September 2009 cover of *The New Yorker* magazine captures the changing roles of students and adults with technology. In the image, a student, no older than 10 or 11, stands at the front of a classroom, writing "text speak" on an old-fashioned chalkboard. Groupings of letters and symbols, such as "G2G," "BTW," "<3," and "BFF" cover the chalkboard. An audience of tuned-out adults sits at their desks, shown side-talking, fully engaged in the kind of distraction many teachers today bemoan in the digital natives' generation. The message is clear. Kids and adults are speaking different languages when it comes to technology, and kids and adults cannot figure out how to engage each other with technology.

Can you speak their language? Test your Text Speak.

Can you decode these messages?

LOL • UOK • IDK • OMG • G2G • BTW • IMHO • <3 • FWIW • ROFL • BFF • THX • F2F • B4N • SOS • 121 • IIRC • l33t

"I totally pwned teh test!!11one!! Can 1 CU F2F B4 PE?"

In this "language," numbers are often used in place of vowels, so 3s are Es, 4 is a stand-in for "fore," and common typos are embraced—teh=the, pwned=owned, which is slang for bested, as in a game, haczOr=hacker, 1=!=l, one=1=!

---

*Laugh out loud **or** lots of love • You okay? • I don't know •
Oh my gosh • Got to go • By the way • In my humble opinion
(never used humbly) • Love/friendship (sideways heart) •
For what it's worth • Rolling on the floor laughing •
Best friends forever • Thanks • Face to face • Bye for now •
Standing over shoulder (e.g., parent) • One to one
(private chat) • If I recall/remember correctly •
Leet/Elite*

*"I totally owned (bested, beat) the test!!!!!!!! Can I see you face to
face before PE?"*

But what if there were a school where every teacher was required to run courses on Facebook? Many schools have pushed teachers to have their own websites with syllabi, unit samples, and topical web links. But the missing piece of such efforts is the lack of interaction for the user. Facebook forces interaction and active learning. It has speed and multitasking wrapped into one page. One teacher with whom I have spoken says just this: "Students multitask and we need to create classrooms that multitask." This particular teacher has given her classroom a facelift, and she teaches the class essentially online. YouTube videos, Google images, and iTunes songs plaster her PowerPoint lectures, and she posts daily to a class blog and includes interactive features in her homework assignments. Students love her class, and they rarely get sidetracked as they take notes on their laptops and input data during hands-on labs. This teacher's premise is to make the classroom mirror the online lives of the students so that students will not be distracted from educational goals. She has never had a technology-related discipline issue in her class. Imagine what this teacher could do with a school-sanctioned Facebook page. Her already innovative approach would expand exponentially.

In their March 2009 article in *Educational Leadership*, Urs Gasser and John Palfrey, coauthors of the book *Born Digital: Understanding the First Generation of Digital Natives*, ask the critical question for schools regarding multitasking:

> Should we expend all our effort in trying to prevent digital natives from multitasking? The answer is no. … What we suggest, therefore, is engaging in a structured conversation with digital natives about multitasking as one strategy that can help them cope with the sea of information. An understanding of the way multitasking challenges learning can even help students practice intentional learning and thus improve the performance of their working memory. (p. 18)

The virtue of the online classroom is that it does not require classroom walls. Learning goes on 24/7, and with the right curriculum design, students will want to spend their time outside of school collaborating and adding content to class Facebook pages, for example. The teacher who created the 20th-century China assignment shared that her students added to their class-created Facebook pages at every hour of the day and night. Motivation skyrocketed, and learning grew more authentic with this real-time audience.

Dale Dougherty, editor and publisher of *Make Magazine*, spoke at Nueva in May 2009. He has likened the schools of the future to a wild ecosystem. Students are growing up in a jungle, he argues, and schools need to figure out how to make sense of the "wild." One productive way to do this is to develop a giant, two-way "smart" grid to disseminate information and facilitate communication through student-developed Facebook pages, where key educational interests and accomplishments are posted and shared. Current project work can then grow more quickly and deeply with collaboration across states, countries, and continents, Dougherty explains. One key question schools need to begin to ask is, "What is the enrollment at school beyond school walls?"

Jeff Jarvis, in his book *What Would Google Do?*, poses the ultimate challenge for schools:

> Perhaps we need to separate youth from education. Education lasts forever. Youth is the time for exploration, maturation, socialization. ... What if we told students that, like Google engineers, they should take one day a week or one course a term or one year in college to create something: a company, a book, a song, a sculpture, an invention? School could act as an incubator, advising, pushing, and nurturing their ideas and effort. What would come of it? Great things and mediocre things. But it would force students to take greater responsibility for what they do and to break out of the straitjacket of uniformity. (p. 212)

Schools can offer programming electives to interested students and channel their energies to produce authentic products. One eighth grade student at Nueva devoted a year of study to developing an iPhone application. He worked with his father, a programmer, and when he hit a bump, he sought out advice from some of Apple's finest and linked up with mentors in the programming field. Far more hours were spent tinkering on this project than would have occurred during a regular course of study, and the more schools can unleash this type of creative energy in students, the faster and more productive these students will become in a rapidly changing work culture. As the *New York Times* reported (April 3, 2009), the "iPhone Gold Rush" is on. In fall 2008, Stanford University offered an undergraduate course called iPhone Application Programming that attracted 150 students for only 50 spots.

We live in a "flat" world, as Friedman has argued. This "flatness" extends into the field of education. The old hierarchical model of education needs to be dismantled in favor of cross-platform teaching and learning. We can't afford to wait to do this, and, more importantly, kids can't wait for us. A provocative video posted on YouTube (October 21, 2008) on the progression of information technology, "Did You Know?" (www.youtube.com/ watch?v=cL9Wu2kWwSY), states:

> We are currently preparing students for jobs that don't yet exist using technologies that haven't been invented in order to solve problems we don't even know are problems yet.

Now is the time for full-scale reconsideration of instructional delivery with the latest technology tools. As stated in the 2008 MacArthur Foundation study on digital youth, *Living and Learning with New Media: Summary of Findings from the Digital Youth Project:*

> They [kids] are often more motivated to learn from peers than from adults. ... To stay relevant in the 21st century, education institutions need to keep pace with the rapid changes introduced by digital media.

Of course, social networking and Facebook do not come without certain caveats. Schools are increasingly trapped in a Gordian knot with the onslaught of the Facebook age. The boundaries between home and school are so twisted that school administrators, parents, and students find themselves caught between them. To untangle this knot, all three groups need to come together to communicate about fair play. The news of Katherine Evans and her lawsuit against Pembroke Pines Charter High School in Pembroke Pines, Florida, highlight the challenges of untying this knot. Suspended from school for creating a Facebook page aimed at venting frustration at the actions of her high school English teacher, the student, along with the American Civil Liberties Union (ACLU), cried foul at perceived first amendment violations. The school crouched under the desk of its legal counsel. This problem will only grow worse unless all parties can create an agreement for fair play at home and in school. Kids will not cease posting on Facebook, and the faster schools and parents can grasp that reality, the healthier the lives of students will be.

The question centers on how to build a bridge that connects students, parents, and schools. The Common Sense Media (CSM) schools program can serve as a starting point for such a project. Founded five years ago as a nonpartisan organization committed to media safety for kids and families, CSM has launched a schools program, with over 4,000 participating schools. CSM has national reach and is one of the few organizations committed to making online living harmonious for kids, families, and now schools. CSM offers practical resources and lesson ideas for educators and conducts workshops, presentations, and focus groups with students and teachers for schools.

CSM even has a family media agreement. In *Born Digital*, Urs Gasser and John Palfrey (2008) write:

> Young people—especially those who are Digital Natives—are themselves setting the norms for how they share information, and these norms may or may not turn out to be a positive influence or to protect them sufficiently from harm. Since parents and teachers have not yet figured out how to deal with these same issues, it could be time for a dialogue. There is an enormous opportunity for Digital Natives and their parents to listen to one another and to establish shared, positive norms regarding

privacy issues as we move forward in the digital age. (pp. 63–64)

Parent education evenings can serve as a starting point for this dialogue and can underscore for parents the benefits of reaching out to a community for guidance and support. Oftentimes, parents feel they are alone as they figure out how to create boundaries at home. As one Nueva parent put it:

> When my son has "homework time," unless I am actually looking at his computer screen to make sure he is working on homework, he is either IMing or playing an Internet war game. This is a very frustrating and concerning situation for me as a parent. I need the tools to monitor his use effectively. At home, much of his computer time for schoolwork is spent off task.

Schools can work with parents to develop mutually beneficial and reinforcing terms of use and brainstorm strategies for effective monitoring at home. Some schools have even gone so far as to create a list of acceptable behaviors on Facebook and on the Internet in general. Parents do not want to feel alone, and they should not have to if schools can figure out with them how to balance the exciting features of social networking with the need for safe structures for teens.

My sister offers an excellent case in point. She asked me "to friend" her 16-year-old son on Facebook last year because she was worried about what he was doing. She figured, correctly, that her son would be more inclined to friend his uncle than his own mother. Sure enough, I became one of my nephew's friends, and I periodically check his page to make sure his postings do not sink into the pit of locker-room language. Of course, what a 16-year-old deems inappropriate is quite different from my own sensibilities as a school administrator. However, I did teach high school students for seven years, so I have a pretty good idea of the line between cool and out of bounds.

School administrators struggle with transgressions after school hours and outside of school networks. When unhealthy online activity takes place in homes and on weekends, the aftereffects often ripple through schools and affect peer relationships during the day. Schools can raise parental awareness through conversations and information sharing, but the trickier issue is whether to impose discipline on students for inappropriate and unsafe cyberactions outside of school. Now, with lawsuits looming, even more schools will cower at the prospect of disciplining student actions on Facebook and other social networking sites for fear of reprisal.

Schools can put their heads in the sand and ignore the problem. They can draw a line in the sand, with zero tolerance rules written into school handbooks, or they can shift with the changing sands of social networking and seek solutions to incorporate social networking and utilize it as part of the educational program for students. We have reached the tipping point here, and schools must address and embrace the prodigious energy surrounding the Facebook age.

If schools block Facebook use on campus, students have no opportunity to integrate social networking into their learning environment and are, instead, left to swim alone in what can be treacherous waters. When problems arise, often after hours and even late into the night, schools face the fallout in the hallways. Students carry the burdens of unhealthy Facebook exchanges with them throughout the school day.

It is time to unravel the knot of conflict between students and schools and disentangle the web of lawsuits that could easily overtake the better measure of capitalizing on the cooperation and communication that the Facebook age brings to educational settings.

Parents are aching for guidance, and the more effectively home and school can partner, the better off communities will be. One parent commented:

With a son in high school, I've had a lot of opportunity to think about Facebook and the issues it presents, which are certainly complex. Although I continue to have mixed feelings about the whole phenomenon, Facebook is—for all intents and purposes—unavoidable in high school. However, I really don't think it's unavoidable in middle school. Because we believe that part of what students learn in middle school is to organize themselves and be responsible and independent about their work, we don't allow our daughter to have a Facebook page. It's just too tempting and too time-consuming, and there is so much other stuff on which we would like to see her spending time. Furthermore, the issues about privacy, sensitivity, and good judgment are complicated, and somewhat challenging for a middle schooler to navigate gracefully.

This parent is begging for guidance from the school. Clear boundaries exist at home, but the concern over how much and how soon a student should enter the Facebook age has this parent searching for answers. She goes on to ask the school to take a stance on Facebook accounts in middle school:

Anyway, I know that the school is not—nor should it be—in a position to tell families what to permit in their homes. However, I wonder if parents would be at all receptive to a strong recommendation from the school that kids hold off on having Facebook pages until they leave middle school. Maybe the horse has already left the barn on this one—or maybe you don't agree with me!—but I think that if you do share my concerns, it might be worth considering whether the school wants to take an official stance on this.

What is interesting about this parent's comment is that she is not alone in her request. She is not abdicating responsibility for managing her child at home. She is just asking for a unified voice between home and school. This is not unreasonable.

However, students are not ready for this to happen, and, in fact, putting a full-scale ban on Facebook runs counter to all of the current research that highlights the meteoric rise of Facebook use among teens. Project Tomorrow, the Irvine, California–based organization that sponsors an annual survey of students, teachers, parents, and administrators, saw a 150% increase between 2007 and 2008 in the proportion of students using social-networking sites (such as Facebook) to work with their peers on group projects for school.

One parent noted the oddity of a school, particularly a middle school, endorsing Facebook use, given that the Facebook user agreement prohibits children below the age of 13 from joining. He writes:

> The terms-of-service for Facebook state you have to be 13+ years old and in high school. Now we both know people routinely lie about this, but does a school want to encourage this?

One 11-year-old student shared that she asked her mother about joining Facebook and explained that she had to be 13 to get an account. Her mother told her to just say she was 14 and sign up. The student presented the story as a routine matter and not one to deter her from social networking.

Beyond the widespread use of social networking among teens, there is a vast gulf separating students and adults in terms of understanding the culture created by the phenomenon. Adults (ages 30 and over) are often appalled at the colorful language students use on Facebook and are unable to wrap their heads around how flippant students can be on their Facebook walls, which are open to public view. When asked about this behavior, students look at the adults as if they have three heads. One student responded:

> I know I swear on Facebook, but everyone I know swears on Facebook. My friends are not offended by my posts.

Schools are not obligated to censor student use of Facebook, especially when Facebook is not accessible on many campuses, but schools do have a responsibility to alert parents when the school becomes aware of student missteps on Facebook.

But just when school communities think they have a handle on Facebook and social networking in general, a new issue develops that brings fear back to the surface. For example, Facebook's "bathroom wall" feature invites users to post anonymous comments in a public space, and other users can add to the posts. The comments can get nasty and dirty pretty quickly, and the worst part about this feature is that only friends can post the anonymous comments about friends. It is this kind of feature, not developed by Facebook by the way, that strikes fear into the hearts of parents, and, understandably, makes parents want to limit their children's access to social networking.

Ira Glass, in a *This American Life* episode on National Public Radio, entitled "The Cruelty of Children" (August 21, 2009), has a conversation with a first grader about bullies. They were on a school bus, and he asked the first grader what kind of books he takes out of the library. The student then opened up and shared that the "bully kid" takes out the "bully" books from the library. Glass, filled with incredulity, asks the child why anyone would write a book that showed the good side of a bully. Glass looked into this with teachers and parents at the school and was unable to find any books that endorsed bullying behavior. But in the child's mind, this was a very real fear—that there were books in libraries that taught children how to be bullies. The challenge posed by social networking tools and online programs is that people involved with them can and do create tools that allow for bullying and unkind behavior, such as the "bathroom wall" feature on Facebook. That is the ugly side of the Internet. Schools and parents need to work together to mitigate the harmful effects such unregulated content can bring to children.

At Nueva, we continue to block access to Facebook on campus, more to the dismay of faculty than students, since the age restrictions limit users under the age of 13 from getting an account. That, of course, is no hurdle for middle school students who really want to have a Facebook account. There is an easy way to bypass the school's content blockage, one parent shares. She just uses her mobile phone to access her Facebook page when she is on campus.

 Who blocks Facebook?

Facebook has encountered a lot of controversy. Schools such as Nueva aren't alone in blocking Facebook. According to Wikipedia, entire countries have banned Facebook intermittently, including Iran, China, Vietnam, and Syria. Facebook "has also been banned at many places of work to discourage employees from wasting time using the service" ("Facebook," Wikipedia).

Read more at http://en.wikipedia.org/wiki/Facebook/.

At this point at Nueva, the alumni office is the only area where Facebook is being used regularly. There, the alumni director has started to use Facebook to reconnect with the school's alumni network. This is a great way to leverage Facebook to revive the "undead past," as Peggy Orenstein describes in a piece in the *New York Times Magazine* (March 10, 2009, "Growing Up on Facebook"):

> Facebook, after all, is the best evidence yet of the undead past. Ever since I signed up a couple of months ago, I have felt thrust into a perpetual episode of "This Is Your Life" (complete with commercials). "Friends" from nursery school have resurfaced.

Orenstein captures the sentiment of the "oldsters" on Facebook:

> It could be that my generation was the anomalous one,
> that Facebook marks a return to the time when people
> remained embedded in their communities for life, with
> connections that ran deep, peers who reined them in if
> they strayed too far from the norm, parents who expected
> them to live at home until marriage (adult children are
> already reclaiming their childhood rooms in droves).

Orenstein rightly wonders, though, whether young people will stay on Facebook or "find something new: something still unformed, yet to be invented—much like themselves." She may be right.

There are signs that a "Facebook Exodus" may be imminent, writes Virginia Heffernan in the New York Times Magazine (August 26, 2009): "While people are still joining Facebook and compulsively visiting the site, a small but noticeable group are fleeing—some of them ostentatiously." Heffernan wonders whether Facebook might be "doomed to someday become an online ghost town, run by zombie users who never update their pages and packs of marketers picking at the corpses of social circles they once hoped to exploit? Sad, if so." It could be that Facebook users are like kids, just growing tired of the "new toy."

At Nueva, though, we have seen no trends among middle school students that indicate a Facebook exodus. In fact, if anything, we have seen an aging down of Facebook, with students as young as sixth graders having accounts with parental approval.

An article in the New York Times asked, "Is Facebook Growing Up Too Fast?" (March 28, 2009). The more appropriate question to ask is whether schools are evolving too slowly to deal with Facebook and social networking. The pedagogical possibilities these tools can offer are profound, and the opportunity to provide social and emotional guidance to students and their families in their use of Facebook must be broached. There exists a unique moment to better align students and adults, especially with the mushrooming of Facebook use by the "older" generation. Facebook has more than 200 million users, and the longer we all wait to engage, instead of spurning, Facebook in school communities, the worse off students, families, and educators will be. Plus, I don't want my son to miss out on the "iPhone Gold Rush."

chapter 3

iTunes schools

Customized Learning
for the 21st Century

Just as iTunes has changed the way we consume music by making custom playlists available, ubiquitous computing offers schools the opportunity to customize learning for each student.

One of the best educational experiences I ever encountered as a student was the semester I spent at the University of Sussex in Brighton, England, during my junior year abroad. At Sussex, the 16th-century tutorial model was followed: class sizes were two to three students, and I could choose to study in areas that matched my passions and interests. As part of a history course on Elizabethan England, for example, I traveled to London to attend performances of plays that appeared on the reading list I had developed with the professor, and I received extensive, timely feedback on my writing. This was in 1989.

Twenty years later, with the explosion of online learning, the opportunity to customize and individualize learning is more than possible and should fast become the mandate of every school system in the United States. Although the possibility of reducing class sizes to two to three students is not realistic, the idea that we might tailor learning to the needs and interests of each student is no longer far-fetched.

Steve Lohr writes in a *New York Times* article about the "School of One" (September 12, 2009): "Today, though, 21st-century technology carries the potential to nudge mainstream education back toward the 16th-century vision of 1-to-1 tutoring."

There is hope, and it could be just around the corner. At the School of One, a pilot program in New York City, individualization and customization are the order of the day. Setting up "flight boards" on screens in the classroom, students find out what their daily departure and itinerary look like. Instead of attempting to herd the whole class, the teacher moves individual students at their own pace, using different online activities and assessments. Some students work in small groups and collaborate. In the *New York Times* article, "Laptop? Check. Student Playlist? Check. Classroom of the Future? Check" (July 21, 2009), New York City Schools Chancellor Joel Klein states, "We're looking in a way that I don't think anyone has looked at—at the way children learn, pacing them at their own pace, all of it tied to the mastery of content and skill and achievement."

However, after I shared my excitement about the School of One approach to learning with one longtime math educator, he worried that the students in the program were essentially just doing glorified worksheets on the computers. And, my wife, a first grade teacher, commented, "You see what's wrong with this, don't you—where's the face-to-face, human contact?" Both have valid points. To be at its most effective, 1-to-1 laptop learning still relies on interpersonal connections to forge strong relationships among students and between students and teachers. The passing of Frank McCourt and the subsequent flood of notes from his students, who shared tales of their deep, lasting relationships with the legendary Stuyvesant educator, only underscore the impact a great teacher can have on students. This has nothing to do with technology; instead, it's about being what psychologist Robert Brooks has termed the "charismatic adult" for students. No matter how many bells and whistles schools come up with to engage students so that they will not be "bored" anymore, at the end of the day, learning will happen best in the presence of dynamic adults who are open to listening to students and their ideas about their own learning.

At Nueva, highly gifted math students participate in a program called Independent Study Math. The goal of the program is to let students move at their own pace and to allow them, in conjunction with an adult mentor/teacher, to direct their learning. For example, Independent Study Math students are encouraged to pursue specific areas of passion inside of math, such as Euclidian geometry. The teacher of the class is a graduate of Nueva and a mathematician. The school is fortunate to have him, not only because he exemplifies Brooks's description of the charismatic adult, but also because he is taking advantage of 1-to-1 laptop learning to feed the interests and skills of his students.

Using an online math program called ALEKS (Assessment and Learning in Knowledge Spaces; www.aleks.com), this teacher has employed individualized learning to help students move at their own pace outside of regular class meetings. As stated on its website, ALEKS "provides the advantages of 1-on-1 instruction, 24/7, from virtually any web-based computer for a fraction of the cost of a human tutor." Tapping into a program like ALEKS has completely transformed his approach to teaching this class and to thinking about how to individualize the program for each student. Having kids use ALEKS frees up class time for the deeper level discussions, but this teacher can track student progress with the assessment tools ALEKS provides.

He does not yet view ALEKS as a replacement for the course content. Instead, he sees the program as an additional teaching tool to further customize learning for his students.

One of his math colleagues, however, is not convinced that a program like ALEKS is the way to go. He worries that students will focus their energies on the more rote method that ALEKS emphasizes and thus be less inclined to adopt alternative ways to learn math topics. ALEKS cannot operate as a substitute for learning at the hands of a skilled questioner. The teacher is the critical piece in the puzzle of modular online learning tools like ALEKS. Fortunately, at Nueva, we have skilled teachers who understand the importance of balancing online programs with the more nuanced pedagogy of complex problem-solving discussions. It would not be prudent for schools to adopt a program such as ALEKS to act as a stand-alone course or substitute for face-to-face interaction in a rich math classroom learning environment.

The upside of a program like ALEKS is that it enables students to continue with math outside of class, at a pace and with feedback tailored to their ability levels. This type of "modular" learning consists of having students work outside the classroom by reading or processing some sort of online learning, in this case through ALEKS; classroom time can then be devoted to activities and practice. A dynamic, knowledgeable teacher is still needed to steer the direction of the learning, though this individual may act more as a learning coach than a traditional sage on the stage.

One talented writing teacher, also a Nueva graduate, sees the possibilities of the School of One approach and has planned his curriculum with the model in mind. After I shared the New York Times article about the School of One with him, he commented:

> I really enjoyed picturing this classroom while reading the article. Yes, I love the idea of individualized paths through a single classroom experience—and the idea that the customization is computerized is fascinating (if harder to imagine for writing as opposed to math, of course). I also have a bit of an obsession with flying, so I have to admit I was especially taken with the idea of the airport traffic pattern seating arrangements and the flight schedule

displays for student tasks. I'm just starting to plan some new curriculum, so this has me thinking about some inventive "itineraries" for future classes.

In *Disrupting Class: How Disruptive Innovation Will Change the Way the World Learns* (2008), Clayton Christensen outlines ways in which schools can move to customized, individualized classrooms. Christensen states:

> Student-centric learning opens the door for students to learn in ways that match their intelligence types in the places and at the paces they prefer by combining content in customized sequences. As modularity and customization reach a tipping point, there will be a change: teachers will serve as professional learning coaches and content architects to help individual students progress—and they can be a guide on the side, not a sage on the stage. (p. 39)

Technology and online courses offer one avenue to explore. With the increasing popularity of the virtual classroom, teachers can mine successful programs and seek ways to implement them into the course of study. Teachers can begin by looking at Florida's Virtual Schools (FLVS), which Christensen discusses. In the April 2009 issue of *Education Next*, a publication of the Hoover Institution at Stanford, Bill Tucker provides an in-depth look at the Florida model. The FLVS motto is "Any time, any place, any path, any pace." The model employs a variety of teaching methods "to engage students, including live 1-to-1 or small group virtual whiteboard sessions, asynchronous discussion, and even a new experimental, immersive online game for an American history course."

In California, Governor Arnold Schwarzenegger is trying to get the state to replace high school science and math texts with free, open source digital versions. The California Free Digital Textbook Initiative's call for customized textbooks, or flexbooks, invites teachers to develop their own modules to use with students. They can pool resources from multiple open source texts to customize materials for their class and even outfit individual students with their own personalized text (which can also include video and music sources). Teachers must create a "customized" solution for each student.

Neeru Khosla, former Nueva School parent and founder of CK–12 (www.ck12.org/flexr/), producer of flexbooks, comments in the *New York Times* ("In a Digital Future, Textbooks Are History," August 8, 2009):

> The good part of our flexbooks is that they can be anything you want. You can use them online, you can download them onto a disk, you can print them, you can customize them, you can embed video. When people get over the mind-set issue, they'll see that there's no reason to pay $100 a pop for a textbook, when you can have the content you want free.

With the increasing availability of university lectures online through YouTube EDU, teachers can also tap into the expertise of lecturers at places such as MIT, Stanford, and Harvard to enrich learning opportunities for students. Teachers should consider developing a yearlong independent project concept for each student and have students work outside of the regular curriculum on an area they are passionate about. In addition, students could be encouraged to find mentors to help them work through their projects.

At Nueva, eighth grade students participate in just such a project, called the Mentored Recital Project, a yearlong investigation into a topic of interest and passion. More and more students are moving toward technology-based projects, with iPhone programming taking the lead in student interest. As the school is fortunate to have so many programmers in its midst, our students can find mentors, meet with them, learn the programming language, and begin to engage their passions around a real world problem. However, given the nature of the global marketplace, mentorship does not need to be contained within the walls of the school community. One Nueva parent who develops applications for the iPhone says that he has never met the programmer who writes the language for his applications. The developer lives in India. With 1-to-1 learning and videoconferencing, why couldn't students work with a mentor on the other side of the globe?

Customization is already prevalent in our culture. We are all using iTunes for music downloads, podcasts, and games. The beauty of iTunes is that it allows us to individualize our purchases: instead of having to download an entire album, we can pick out the songs we like best, grab them with one or two clicks, and import them into our mobile devices. With the advent of free resources like Hulu, which offers streaming video of TV shows and movies, and Pandora, a personalized Internet radio service, customization has also become cost-effective, a huge plus in this day of ever-shrinking school budgets, particularly in states like California. Schools need to find a way for teachers and students to take advantage of these opportunities. Imagine if teachers and students had a virtual one-stop shop where they could go to download a poem, a work of art, a physics problem, a science lab, or a video lecture by a leading expert in the field! Teachers would then take on the role of Ms. Frizzle from the children's series *The Magic School Bus*. Acting as navigators for students, teachers would transport them into different lands of learning.

With the advent of the Kindle and the iPhone, laptop computers will soon become passé. Kids can and should be able to tap into a customized learning network to enhance, not replace, their academic program. Teachers could then individualize work in and outside class to reach and challenge students of all ability levels more effectively. The biggest challenge is figuring out how to harness the vast array of resources available, but the task is too complex for teachers and schools to do alone. Kids are trapped at desks when they should be getting up and moving knowledge around fluently, with support and guidance from their teachers.

At iTunes U, which is part of the iTunes Store, we find more than 200,000 audio and video files, such as free lectures and other high-level content from universities such as Stanford and Indiana, among many others. It is beginning to turn traditional textbook learning on its head. The limitation with iTunes U is that it is geared primarily toward university students. There should be a clearinghouse for K–12 educators to share and distribute their best materials for free download. Fortunately, iTunes U is beginning to tap into K–12 learning and has started to collect content for sharing among K–12 teachers and schools. Teachers no longer have to work in isolation, within the walls of their schools; instead, they can be content creators and contributors, with places to go to pull the best resources to use with their students. Once they have all of this information at their fingertips, though, they need to begin to make sense of it for students. This can be overwhelming.

Some educators have already started to play with iTunes U for the K–12 environment. In an article at *Edutopia*, "In One Ear: iTunes Puts iPods to Good Use," Maya Payne Smart (2008) mentions one AP math teacher who "makes up to five videos a week in which he solves math problems or answers student questions." This is a great first step, but teachers need to go a step further and construct customized programs for each student. The monolithic, standards-based approach to teaching has to disappear. It is exciting for the teacher to incorporate these materials into a class presentation on a topic, but the learning that takes place outside of class, when students can explore and learn on their own, is really where iTunes U can help students. The picture: a student comes into a class, brimming with excitement at having posted a puzzling math homework problem to a math forum to seek help from experts in the field to figure out a way to solve the problem, and he actually receives suggestions and tips to watch a related instructional video on iTunes U that then enables him to go back and solve the problem on his own. We want to create independent learners, and we now have the tools to better guide students toward full ownership of their learning.

If iTunes U were to link up with the Florida Virtual School model, school could then become a giant playlist, as in the School of One model. Playlists allow users to group songs together so they can find them more quickly and play a specific set of songs. Playlists can be manually or automatically assembled from a library based on specific criteria. Shifting this model to school communities reveals how schools might move toward customization. Under a Playlist model, teachers would work with their students to create meaningful, shared, collaborative learning modules. There would still be content wrapped in, but it would be shaped around a skill and interest set that inspires students to the point that it becomes "cool to be smart," as they develop and add to playlists.

Music sites have already developed the tools that could enable this to happen, and there is no reason education should wait to use them. At Playlist.com, the mission is "to help find and enjoy music legally throughout the web in the same way other search engines help find web pages, images, and other media," and the site makes it easy to "create playlists, share playlists with friends, and browse playlists of others." The field of education could easily co-opt this model to expedite the transmission of knowledge and best practices. Teachers could add to their playlists (which would essentially serve as lesson, unit, or program ideas), and utilize social networks to quickly broaden their repertoire and better serve the needs of their students. Students across disciplines, school districts, states, and even countries could share their playlists and cooperatively customize learning. Students could be graded and evaluated by the quality of their playlists and by the number of hits their playlists get. The same could apply to teachers. School would no longer be trapped inside hallways or classroom walls, and every child could zoom ahead.

Besides allowing students to work at their own pace and giving them access to charismatic experts and teachers around the world, computer-enhanced learning provides a great opportunity for collaborative learning around real-world, real-time problems. Students are not bound to a classroom anymore: the ease and speed of computer-aided communication provides access to experts, mentors, and other students around the world. The story of the Netflix competition to improve the online movie rental service's movie recommendation system highlights the power that can be unleashed when people are allowed to engage with a real problem that needs fixing (not in the "ending global hunger" kind of way, but in the "makes life easier for me" kind of way). The contest began in October 2006 and ended in a dead heat in July 2009 between two teams (*New York Times*, "Netflix Competitors Learn the Power of Teamwork," July 27, 2009). The reason the competition yielded so much success was because it brought people with complementary skills together to combine different methods of problem-solving. Also, the most successful teams were made up of individuals across the globe, illustrating how quickly, efficiently, and collaboratively problems can be attacked and solved.

What if companies like Netflix, Google, Amazon, iTunes Store, Twitter, and so forth pooled their problems—not the top-secret, ready-to-bend-the-market secrets, but the daily puzzles that their software engineers, marketing and communication departments wrestle with every day—and made them available to schools and students to solve? Schools across the globe could engage in the great race to solve real problems that real companies are pouring their resources into figuring out. The Netflix contest fast became "a race to agglomerate as many teams as possible," David Weiss, a PhD candidate in computer science at the University of Pennsylvania told the *New York Times* (July 27, 2009). Students could reach out through Twitter and Facebook to collaborate across skill sets and interest levels to attack with lightning speed and full engagement the problems of the 21st century. How exciting this would be! The question is, would these giant companies open themselves up and allow students access to their problems? We hear all the time the power of "free" with the Internet and open-source software; now, let's see these companies live up to their word. All of Google's tools are free; shouldn't their problems be as well?

Now, let's return to the School of One model with its flight departures and itineraries, and we can begin to see where personalized, paced, and peer-to-peer learning can lead. Schools should replicate the online marketplace and prepare students for their futures. There is a golden opportunity to do so right now: iTunes customization can break open the 21st century and bring the 16th-century tutorial back into being for every child. As reporter Steve Lohr writes (*New York Times*, September 12, 2009):

> One-to-one tutoring is the learning method proven time and again to sharply improve a student's measured performance. A good human tutor can deliver a "home run," educationally and statistically, explained Christopher J. Dede, a professor of education at Harvard University.

At Nueva, what we have seen is that learning environments where 1-to-1 learning is developing clearly enhance student learning and interest, but only in the hands of a "charismatic" adult. Professor Dede uses a critical word, "human," in his explanation of 1-to-1 tutoring and student performance. Great schools and great teaching and learning happen when teachers are always ready to engage the potential in their students and find every way imaginable to tap into their interests, passions, and abilities. No matter the resource used—whether ALEKS, iTunes, or flexbooks—student performance will only improve if the curricular program is carefully constructed, managed, and executed with the individual needs of each student held closely in mind.

In *The Art of Possibility* (2002), Boston Philharmonic conductor Benjamin Zander shares a wonderful parable to illustrate how people can shift their mindsets so that they can see opportunity instead of becoming trapped in a defeated outlook. Two shoe salesmen head to a part of rural Africa to explore the viability of establishing a new market for their shoes. One salesman writes back to the company, "Situation hopeless. No one wears shoes. Abandon project." The other salesman sees the flip side and writes, "No one is wearing shoes. Opportunity abounds. Huge market awaits. Send resources immediately." The same sort of thinking needs to enter the discussion in schools to help teachers and administrators see the possibilities instead of the pitfalls of 1-to-1 learning and to encourage them to harness the vast array of resources now readily available to transform teaching and learning for students. It has to be the hope of every educator that when teachers are exposed to new ideas, they will have the kind of response the Nueva writing teacher had when exposed to the School of One model—one of imagination and vision. Schools will always need great teachers, and all students deserve to have the opportunity to receive individual attention to develop their learning paths in the hands of a master teacher. As more opportunities and resources are available to make this happen every day in every school, teachers would be remiss if they passed up the chance to seize the mantle of 1-to-1 learning. It is the job of school administrators to open this window for teachers and students.

There is no reason to wait on customized learning for students. As soon as tomorrow, students should be able to open their iTunes accounts, see math and writing prompts combined with science labs, songs, and poems, all catalogued according to their interests, abilities, and passions.

chapter 4

kids online
Lying as the New Social Norm?

Again, balancing safety and access is a tricky task,
and some of the solutions involve thorny ethical
dilemmas. To protect kids, do we really want to
encourage them to lie about who they are online?

S ince when did lying become the new social norm? If you walk into any school today and ask students if they have a fake identity online, chances are that 90% or more will raise their hands. When asked why they lie online, many give the answer that they do not want "weird" people to know who they are. Others enjoy the game of identity creation, while still others want to skirt age restrictions and happily fill out online registration forms with false ages. "It's just a number," one student says. The ethical implications of such thinking for educators and parents are huge. Are kids learning that lying is the new social norm? Well, in the words of one educator, "At least they are smart enough to know that they shouldn't share their personal information online."

How should parents and educators even begin to tackle this dilemma? One prudent way, according to one student, is to let kids know that while adults trust them, it's the rest of the world that is the problem. When adults impose restrictions on kids, particularly those related to online activity, kids often feel slighted and even disrespected. This is far from the case in most situations. Adults do genuinely worry about kids online, and they want their children to be safe. The problem, though, in the words of one student, is that "adults don't really have a clue about what goes on online." Kids recognize the gap in knowledge and comfort between themselves and the grown-ups, and they actually are sympathetic to adult naiveté.

One creative way to tackle the problem of lying online, according to one particularly savvy student, is to have students create fake profiles in computer class. Then, the class can open the conversation about the ethical issues associated with falsifying personal information, while addressing the soundness of taking this tack in an effort to avoid encounters with dangerous characters. The ironic thing here is that in many ways, it makes sense for kids to lie about their online selves, especially given the risk of encountering predators who infiltrate game and chat sites to connect with vulnerable, unsuspecting young people.

Other kids, out of fear of being kicked out of a guild in World of Warcraft, for example, freely admit to lying about their ages just so they can continue to be a part of a virtual community. The number of online accounts kids use often touches double digits, and kids traverse e-mail, chat, and game sites with amazing ease, not thinking twice about shifting identities from one venue to the next. There is a certain freedom in such detachment, but it can complicate thinking when kids then confront ethical dilemmas in real time. Furthermore, events in the news do not exactly feature ethical decision making, with Bernie Madoff scamming millions with his notorious Ponzi scheme, for example. Kids need role models to help them learn, but in online life, there are no adult role models available, at least, no adult role models who have any kind of "street cred" with kids. That is a scary prospect, particularly concerning the ease with which kids lie online. Just ask any random student in a school how to circumvent school filters to get on Facebook, and you will get a quick reply to check out flitools.com. It is uncanny how quick students are to openly subvert attempts by schools to safeguard their online activity.

One child described her parents as having a policy of "benign neglect" in terms of legislating her online behavior. Many kids think parents have been too "light" on rules and want their parents to "dig deeper" so that schools do not have to get involved in resolving online transgressions. It is not unlike the attitude some parents have regarding alcohol use among teens. Some parents expect teens are going to try alcohol. Allow it in the home so they will do it under the care of a parent, the thinking goes. As long as things do not get too out of control, all is well, in the minds of some parents. The problem with this thinking is that, unlike with alcohol consumption, oftentimes parents do not know when things get out of control for kids online because the parents did not grow up with and are not used to the online world.

Nancy Darling, associate professor of psychology at Oberlin College in Ohio, completed a study to assess the extent of lying in children and teens (Po Bronson, "Learning to Lie," New York, February 10, 2008). Darling discovered that 98% of teenagers have lied to their parents about everything from friends, to dating, and drugs. Adding online activity to the mix makes these numbers grow even more frightening. "When people are typing, they seem to carry around different norms in their head," says Rutgers University professor Terri Kurtzberg, coauthor of the study "Being Honest Online: The Finer Points of Lying in Online Ultimatum Bargaining" (Academy of Management annual meeting, August 2008). This is vital information to digest, especially as parents and educators begin to figure out how to guide kids through the digital landscape. No current studies document the extent to which kids lie online, other than recent Iowa State findings revealing kids lie about the time they play games online. Broad-based information needs to be unearthed, though the truth could unsettle parents and educators.

We know that teen cell phone use is rampant and growing at an exponential rate. The Benenson Strategy Group conducted more than 1,000 online interviews with teens about cell phone use for Common Sense Media. What they found (Greg Toppo, USA Today, June 18, 2009) is staggering.

More than 8 in 10 teens have cell phones, and over half have had them since they were 12 or younger. Teens send 440 texts in an average week, 110 of which are sent during class. Restrictive school policies hardly matter, as 65% of teens use their phones despite school policies. Parents are fooled as well. Only 23% of parents whose kids have cell phones think they are using them during school, while 65% of kids say they use them in school.

In the area of cheating, the findings grow more alarming. Of the 1,013 teens surveyed, 35% admit to cheating at least once with their cell phones. Teens are more likely to say that their friends are cheating than they are, as 65% of teens say they have seen or heard about other people in their school cheating with cell phones.

How do kids do it? They store information on their cell phones to look at during a quiz or test. They text friends about answers during quizzes and tests, which 57% of teens say others at their school have done. And, they take pictures of quiz and test questions with a cell phone to send to friends.

How do they feel about it? Only 41% of teens surveyed say that storing notes or information on a cell phone to look at during a quiz or test is a serious cheating offense. Almost 1 in 4 (23%) don't think it's cheating at all. Similarly, only 45% say texting friends about answers during tests is cheating and a serious offense, while 20% say it's not cheating at all.

Interestingly, kids consider cheating via the Internet a more serious offense than cell phone cheating. However, while teens viewed plagiarism more seriously than other types of cheating, a full third of teens (36%) said that downloading a paper from the Internet was not a serious offense, and 42% said copying text from websites was either a minor offense or not cheating at all.

According to these findings, if schools keep running business as usual, educators and parents will be in trouble. A cartoon in the *New York Times* Week in Review section (August 30, 2009) captured the shifting tide in classrooms. The time-honored assignment for English classes is to have students write an essay or share a story about their summer vacation. In the cartoon, the teacher stands in front of the classroom and presents the weather-beaten assignment for yet another year. One bold student pipes up with, "What, didn't you follow me on Twitter this summer?" The cartoon lands perfectly with its message that students are using different tools to learn, and classrooms need to change to catch up with the times.

In the area of cell phone use and as an antidote to unethical behavior, teachers need to think about ways to incorporate mobile technologies into their teaching. One creative foreign language teacher at Nueva has explored these possibilities and designs scavenger hunts for her students. She writes:

> Students need to call a number and get instructions on where to go. Once there, they have to complete a task or buy something and call the next number to get further instructions. Each student has slightly different instructions to complete the task—to differentiate the assignment. Ideally, this all happens in a Spanish-speaking environment such as the Mission or Redwood City.

She also has students interview Spanish-speaking people in different countries via Skype, and she assigns students to have 1-on-1 conversations with different Spanish-speaking members of the school community.

One very advanced Spanish student regularly videoconferences with a native speaker during Spanish class. This teacher has taken the 1-to-1 laptop program one step further and asks why the school does not move to a mobile device for students, such as an iPhone.

This teacher can easily imagine students with an iPhone on their trip to Spain. In May of their eighth grade year, students in Nueva's Spanish classes go to Spain for a two-week homestay and cultural immersion program. She could see students using iPhones to take photos, make videos, text in Spanish, and post on a blog or social network to share their experiences with their parents and friends back in the United States! She has the vision to see the possibility where students can become artifact collectors, travel agents, artists, videographers, and cultural anthropologists.

The brilliance of this foreign language teacher is her leap to seeing opportunities with technology.

How to create community for children in schools, particularly regarding online social norms, is a rising challenge for educators and parents. It cannot be done in isolation, and it needs to involve the insights and recommendations of kids. They are the digital natives, after all.

The children's film Ice *Age* (2002) opens with Scrat, the saber-toothed squirrel, desperately attempting to scale a giant glacier, while trying to hold onto an acorn. As the squirrel inches his way upward, a crack in the glacier widens, and water begins to shoot out. Scrat plugs the hole with one hand and holds the acorn in the other hand. Then, another crack opens, and another, and another. The squirrel uses his left foot, his right foot, and with no body parts left, puts his mouth over the last hole he can plug. His cheeks swell with water, the glacier finally explodes with full force, and the squirrel is sent flying for miles as water crashes forth. The squirrel bounces up and down and contorts in all directions. Miraculously, the squirrel survives and ends up on dry land, but just when he thinks he can breathe and see clearly, he is squashed by Manny, the wooly mammoth.

This scene from *Ice Age* captures where schools are with technology today. The schools are the squirrel, technology is the glacier, and the acorn is the student. Schools are at a loss as to how to balance the student (the acorn) and plug the glacier (technology) without imploding, like the squirrel. Just when they figure out one new tech tool, a giant new one, in the form of a wooly mammoth, emerges and crushes them. Technology is simply moving too fast. Students pick up new applications and tools every millisecond of the day. There is no point in trying to put stopgap measures in place to slow the pace. Instead, teachers need to figure out fast how to tap into student expertise and passion and create authentic learning experiences with technology. This is no easy task.

Schools can build the tech infrastructure, and, with new programs like Ning, schools can even create portals for safe social networking, but the challenge is how to get teachers actually to use the tools. Blogs, wikis, the Google suite, Skype, and others all offer different and exciting ways to engage students, but these tools are off the radar and out of the comfort level of most teachers who did not grow up immersed in this culture. In a teacher's world, the work required to be tech savvy becomes just one more thing to do, amid an already busy school day filled with lesson planning, assessment, lunch and recess duties, and communication with parents. "It's enough to just stay on top of school e-mail," one veteran teacher lamented.

Students, though, do not even think twice about ubiquitous technology. They flip screens, add widgets, and answer multiple mail accounts all in a matter of seconds. At school, they cook up recipes to circumvent the porous blocking mechanisms schools attempt to put in place. Schools have to take precautionary, protective measures to keep online usage at school safe, but given the nature of the global marketplace, it is unrealistic to think that schools can keep everything out. Instead, schools should capitalize on teachable moments that arise when students encounter hateful language on a blog post or false claims on a website. Examine the intent, explore the bias, strategize a response, and invite the students to develop a solution. Every parent and educator wants students to make sensible decisions when they are on their own out in the world. Students are deprived of precious learning opportunities under the guidance and care of adults who care about them if schools and parents block their online access. Adults end up looking like Scrat the squirrel to the students. This does not inspire trust; instead, it breeds cynicism and drives a deeper wedge between students and adults.

Schools are obligated to cultivate a sense of community, but the nature of that community has changed. Instead of a monolithic, one-size-fits-all approach to blocking and filtering, schools need to articulate a clear approach and customize filtering based on developmental needs of students. No matter how many times schools scramble the Rubik's cube of filtering, students can find their way back in two steps or less. Students can just type "bypassing school filters" into Google and find thousands of how-to guides on the topic. The last thing schools want to do is encourage a game mentality of how many different ways students can come up with to break the filter.

As reported in *Education Week* (May 1, 2009), a survey by the Consortium for School Networking (CoSN) documents that 70% of school districts do not allow access to social networking and chat rooms in school, but they do permit blogging, file sharing, interactive games, and online forums. There is a sea change taking place, but it is slow and deliberate. The report states:

> School districts are only now developing new policies and practices regarding Web 2.0. Most are exploring the potential of Web 2.0 as they seek to build student awareness, keep students safe, and develop a sense of responsibility and rights related to Internet use among students, staff, and community.

One educator, a former colleague of mine from Princeton Day School, hints at why schools are slow to shift their policies. The challenge, he says, is to figure out the culture piece, while moving teachers and students along at a manageable pace so that students do not take the reins of power and drive school culture around technology. He writes:

> We, as teachers, have to get used to some behavior that we used to consider to be unacceptable and how, at the same time, we need to make and enforce rules about behavior involving technology that we truly don't approve of.

Of course, there is not yet common ground between students and teachers on what those appropriate behaviors are. The laptop experience at Nueva only underscores this cultural divide.

The reality for schools is that the technology is not going away. In fact, it is only getting more advanced. The recent demonstration of MIT designers of a sixth sense prototype, with holographic touch screens (www.youtube.com/watch?v=mUdDhWfpqxg), only reinforces the notion that blocks are futile. The design allows users to use their fingers to take pictures, make phone calls, and learn everything about a person they meet for the first time, based on the person's web profile. Images of words aligned with Facebook pages, Google searches, and blog postings layer across the body of the person. Pretty soon, there will be nothing to block. The walls are disappearing.

To avoid the fate of Scrat the squirrel, schools have to change course. The glacier is too big, and it is only getting bigger.

The question centers on the best way to engage students in a dialogue around ethical behavior. Fortunately, Common Sense Media, Project New Media Literacies, and Harvard's Good Play Project have teamed up to develop a dynamic digital life curriculum. In the introduction to the curriculum, Common Sense Media explains: "A successful shift in culture—whether it is about digital ethics, environmental sustainability, or global awareness—requires multiple players and constituencies devoted to the same cause."

Nueva teachers joined Common Sense Media as part of the pilot training for the deployment of these curricular materials. The curriculum was implemented in Nueva's nationally recognized

Social and Emotional Learning (SEL) program, which plays a key role in developing the curriculum at every grade level. As the school's website states:

> The program empowers students to examine their own thoughts and actions and be sensitive to the feelings and needs of others. Within the context of guided activities and peer feedback, SEL gives children the tools to be successful within the interpersonal domain.

In the course of piloting the Good Play curricula, one creative SEL teacher developed his own twist to the materials, engineering a lesson entitled "Step-by-Step: Ethical Decision Making in an Online World." This teacher used his lesson with students as part of the laptop boot-up camp, which is a one-day orientation for the 1-to-1 laptop program offered at Nueva at the start of each school year. Using a variety of scenarios about online activities that have offline consequences, students worked in small teams to create "decision-making trees." For example, one scenario focused on a MySpace posting involving bullying. Students were first asked to figure out what might escalate the situation, such as, for example, an additional posting that would inflame the bullying already going on. They were also asked to devise a solution that would de-escalate the situation, such as telling their parents or an adult about the bullying behavior. Large Post-it paper blanketed tables in the classroom as the students worked in small groups to talk through challenging online scenarios, which ranged from a teacher reading a student's Facebook wall, to the passing around of an inappropriate photo on a social networking site. The energy in the room crackled with analytical, thoughtful decision making, and students genuinely participated in a constructive conversation about ethical online behavior. The mix of tactile, hands-on learning, coupled with real-world scenarios, lifted the lesson to the level of creative problem-solving and community building.

Another skillful SEL teacher linked up with the computer teacher to have eighth grade students design their own web pages using iWeb, which allows users to create their own website, customizing photos, movies, text, and widgets. She wanted to have students think about the kinds of materials they post online, particularly as they begin the process of applying to high schools. Many Nueva students apply to attend independent high schools, and the feedback from high school admissions offices signals that more and more schools are looking at material posted online as a way to gain a fuller picture of each student. The Nueva teacher went back and forth on how much to define the parameters of the assignment: she wanted to give the students freedom to create and innovate, but she also wanted them to be cautious and smart about what they chose to put on their websites. She wanted to create an environment where the lesson of "think before posting" crystallized.

The inspiration for this lesson grew out of a Good Play project called "The Trillion Dollar Footprint," in which students play the role of television producers charged with selecting a contestant for the imaginary reality TV show *Who Wants to Be a Trillionaire?* Students dig through the digital footprint or online profiles of two contestants to determine which candidate holds the most promise in terms of honesty, openness, creativity, and talent. The documents they examine include Facebook pages, blog postings, letters to the editor written by the contestants, and newspaper articles about an aspect of the lives of the contestants. Inside each of these documents lies telling information about the candidates. Students critically analyze the sources of information provided as well as the content shared by each contestant on the web.

This is a highly engaging type of lesson, and students enjoyed a spirited debate about the foolishness of some of the postings of the contestants. One educator questioned the merits of framing the lesson using the values associated with a reality TV show, while another stressed the key point that the follow-up discussion with students after they complete the activity is where the most critical learning takes place. In the hands of a skilled teacher, this type of lesson drives home the idea of the lasting nature of a digital footprint (one of the online documents included was dated eight years earlier) and enables students to think through the ethical implications of posting profile information online. Examining the sample documents reveals dishonesty in one of the contestants, who claims in one place that he is single and in another writes about being married. Students pounce on the idea of whether lying in an online profile should disqualify a contestant, and this brings the discussion back to one of the central ethical dilemmas surrounding digital life—are there times when it is okay to lie online?

Schools have to tackle this issue with students and integrate online ethics into the curriculum. The keep-it-all-out mentality only widens the gulf between adults and students and can become an endless game of cat and mouse for school administrators, teachers, and parents. There are creative solutions and ways to enter into the discussion of online ethics with students. Projects that invite students to create media, with the guidance of a skillful teacher, allow teachers to see how students engage with media and the choices they make in terms of sharing or oversharing information about themselves. Instead of shutting out cell phones, for example, teachers can devise creative ways for students to use them as tools to enhance learning and to avoid the fiasco of students texting under desks or cheating with cell phones on tests. Also, teachers need to build frameworks that help students to deconstruct decisions they make online and to consider how their decisions online play out offline. Schools have to make a commitment to build these lessons into the existing curriculum and devote time to them in their calendars and schedules. There are now wonderful resources available from organizations like Common Sense Media and the Good Play project to make this happen.

chapter 5

smart parenting
in the Facebook Age

When students bring home a school-issued laptop, who sets the home usage rules? We found that parents had a variety of opinions on the topic, and they were more than happy to share them.

When I was in middle school, each spring on the last weekend of the school year I traveled with my father down to Williamsburg, Virginia, for a soccer tournament. The timing of these trips could not have been worse, as they took place on the weekend before final exams. Along with my soccer gear, I lugged my numerous textbooks and notebooks so that I could review between games in our hotel room. This, of course, was not by choice, but my father demanded it of me. While my teammates traipsed off to Busch Gardens amusement park for an afternoon of careening up and down the Rebel Yell, I sat in the hotel room with my father studying! At the time, I hated him for this.

But we would soon dig into the material, and invariably, my father would want to talk about history, one of his passions and soon to be one of my passions. He would pick out a chapter in the book I was reading, and we would just chat about the different people and events, and he would quiz me here and there. Ironically, I don't remember much about any of the soccer games I played on those weekends, but the image of my father sitting on the hotel room floor, flipping through the pages of a ratty old history textbook the size of the phone book, is forever etched into my recollections.

Years later, as I entered the teaching profession, I reminded my father of those special bonding history study sessions. However, amazingly, he did not have any memory of those moments. In fact, when I mentioned it to him on the phone one night, his response was, "What are you talking about?" I responded incredulously, "What do you mean, Dad, don't you remember making me stay in that hotel room in Williamsburg to study for my final exams?" His response: "I don't remember that at all."

As parents and educators, we often do not know what will stick with children. My father had no idea that he had created such a powerful impression on me in his insistence that I study with him. But 30 years later, I can still recall the Williamsburg hotel room with crystal clarity.

The Facebook age demands that parents be present for their children. One child laments that his mother spends more time on her cell phone than in conversation with him. Another child sadly relays that his mother checks her e-mail every second of the day, even during dinner. At Passover Seder, my wife mentioned to me that one of the guests was checking his iPhone and texting throughout the Seder. I had not even noticed as I was sitting across the table from the guest.

The challenge parents face today is not wholly different from the limits our parents put on us 30 years ago. I had friends whose parents let them eat Twinkies and play Atari, but my parents refused to succumb to such "vices." I resented their rules. Today, parents wrestle with whether to let their child get an account on Facebook. They dread the battle if they say "no," and they are not sure how to say "no."

In "The Undercover Parent," an op-ed piece in the New York Times (March 16, 2008), contributor Harlan Coben discusses the irony within this parental paralysis:

> Today's overprotective parents fight their kids' battles on the playground, berate coaches about playing time and fill out college applications—yet when it comes to chatting with pedophiles or watching beheadings or gambling away their entire life savings, then ... then their children deserve independence?

Schools need to help parents find the language to use to speak to their children about limits online. Parents feel alone. Some resent the wave of technology sweeping their children out to sea, while others simply are at a loss when it comes to engaging in conversation with their teenagers, who, naturally and developmentally, are pushing away from them to be more independent. One student states this sentiment perfectly: "I would prefer if my parents minded their own business. My e-mail is my business, and they have no right to it."

However, other students see the value of parental involvement: "I feel very safe online. My father taught me very good Internet strategies when I was very young, so I feel very comfortable when I'm on the Internet." This child's dad should be celebrated for having the conversation about safe Internet use when his child was at a young age. It is important that parents create the family computer culture at home at an early age. The longer they wait, the more difficult it is to draw clear boundaries, and the more resistance they will receive from their children.

Surprisingly, counter to the stereotype of the out-of-touch parent, parents are plugged in to their teens' online life. According to a study by the Pew Internet and American Life Project on teen and parent Internet use, 65% of parents check to see what websites their child views, and 74% know whether or not their child has a social networking site profile (www.pewinternet.org:80/Reports/2007/ Parent-and-Teen-Internet-Use/Data-Memo/Other-findings-about-teens-and-their-parents.aspx?r=1).

Legendary Indiana University basketball coach Bob Knight said that if the chemistry teacher at IU was making an impact on a student and if Knight was struggling to reach that same student, he would go talk to the chemistry teacher to find out what was working. Parents need to do the same. They need to swap stories of success and failure, so they can find the right catching point with their child. Schools can help gather best practices from parents and provide strategy sessions with relevant, provocative scenarios to role-play. They can hold parent evenings and create online forums for parents to vent their frustrations and seek practical solutions. All of this is difficult, but, as Coben says, "Parenting has never been for the faint of heart" (*New York Times*, 2008).

At Nueva, we hold parent media evenings. They are well attended and provide an outlet and a resource for parents who wish to share, strategize, and even agree upon norms of behavior to instill at home. The two Social and Emotional Learning (SEL) teachers who run the evenings are very skilled in facilitating discussion, and they gather data from the students ahead of time to gauge the level and degree of their media use. They then share this data with parents and use it as a springboard to enter into discussion. The response from parents is quite favorable and appreciated. One parent commented:

> I liked the first part, which was data driven and fact based. Really helps ground the conversation. The second part, where you collected the parents' questions to guide the conversation thematically instead of leaving it to random questions, was also great. The session made me think about things I had not been thinking about regarding technology and kids—which is terrific! I think the suggestion

about coming up with a "community view" on IM/Chat, Facebook, such that it is prohibited in certain homework hours, is interesting.

Another way to bring parents together is to have them create a guide of strategies to use at home with their children. At Nueva, at the end of year one of the 1-to-1 program, we enlisted parents to share their stories, and we use these stories at the start of each year with new and returning parents. The topics ranged from how to install parental controls (fear), to engagement and modeling (Facebook or possibility). Much of the advice is powerful, and the fact that it comes from parents who have lived through the program gives the advice credibility and provides reassurance to those whose children are just beginning the laptop program. One parent writes:

> It is my opinion that your attitude about [the laptop program] will directly affect your relationship with your child. You can join with them and ensure they understand your desire to keep them a safe, well-rounded, healthy student, or you can build emotional walls between you on the other extreme. This is one of those things that we don't think about until it has gone sour.

This parent does not want to succumb to fear; instead, he wants to work with his child to create a safe, sane home media environment.

However, many parents struggle with how to begin the conversation about home media use. One parent offers direct advice:

> Determine up front, and explicitly with your child, what privileges of privacy you are giving. You may believe their messages to be solely theirs, like U.S. mail, or you may feel that they are completely public, as they are once they are sent in cyberspace. There is no right or wrong answer, but where you are on this continuum is important to think about and communicate to your child. Will you

require they give you access and then use it to review their messages? Are their messages private until you have a reason to believe that they are getting into trouble? Or hurting someone's feelings? Will you view their messages regularly? Then, whatever you decide, be consistent unless you feel that it is not working, and then be explicit with your child about changing. I've seen hurt feelings as parents vacillate on this privacy issue and children feel personally invaded. Repairing this is hard.

This is thoughtful, engaged parenting at its best.

Another way for parents to learn about and educate their child on safe, appropriate media use is to use the media the child is using. One parent suggests:

Consider engaging with them. E-mail them and ask them things that require a reply to you. If they are IMing, consider having an account and being one of their friends. Consider sending them text messages if they are messaging with others. You will see how they engage. You are showing them by example, and they're probably going to respond to you as they do to others.

Stanford University professor B. J. Fogg, director of the Persuasive Technology Lab, has developed a website called Facebook for Parents. The approach Fogg takes is to focus more on how to think about Facebook than what to do: "Our how-to-think approach empowers parents to deal with whatever comes next." Fogg continues:

Some parents worry about joining Facebook because they don't want to intrude on their child's privacy. They see it as spying in their kid's bedroom. This view—Facebook as private bedroom—is not accurate.

What should parents know about Facebook?

A good starting point for parents is B. J. Fogg's website, Facebook for Parents: www.facebookforparents.org.

And when things go wrong, what should parents do?

For example, a parent sees his child distraught, sitting at the computer. The child is clearly shaken, and the parent walks over to console and talk with the child. The child shares what is on the computer screen, and it sends ripples of fear through the parent. The parent learns that the child is being cyberbullied by a classmate on Facebook. Should the parent contact the school?

Yes. Schools want to know when cyberbullying happens, even if it occurs after school hours and at home. The aftereffects of these incidents can often spread through school the next day and affect the emotional safety of a child. How should parents engage their children with Facebook? One successful way is to become a friend on their Facebook page. But this can be problematic, as *Washington Post* reporter Ruth Marcus explains:

> Parents friending their own children is seen as a particularly unnatural act. As my daughter explained, perfectly pleasantly, "There are things that I talk about with my friends that I don't need you to know." (April 1, 2009)

So, if a child resists friending, parents can ask an uncle or aunt or close relative or family friend to friend the child. I am a friend of my 16-year-old nephew because my sister does not want to be his friend on Facebook. I periodically check in on his Facebook page to see if the content being posted is appropriate. During the summer between his sophomore and junior years, while he was away for a week with two of his friends, I noticed a spike in activity on his Facebook wall, and some of the comments being posted were not appropriate. I wrote to him immediately and asked him to take down the posts. He apologized and took them down right away. There also needs to be an adult presence close by in the event a cyberbullying incident takes place. And the child needs to know that adults are available to help.

However, some parents view overinvolvement as problematic. One parent explains:

> Among adults, there is a collective naiveté about how technology evolves in the youth culture. It is hubris to think that our command of the ever-changing communication landscape is in any meaningful way superior to theirs even at this tender age. History has repeatedly proven us wrong in this regard. Better to teach underlying human values of self-restraint and responsibility towards others than try to close a barn door long left open by the evolving Facebook world.

Schools across the country are wrestling with how and whether to handle student life on Facebook. One school administrator captures the tension:

> The issue of having to deal with Facebook and discipline seems to be coming up more frequently. In particular, the challenge that I find is determining what falls under the school's purview, i.e., where do we draw the line between what is the parent's responsibility and what is the school's responsibility? I would love to know if any of you have any guidelines or policies that deal with this matter.

It is tricky business. Students rightly demand to know how it is the school's business to get involved in what they are doing on Facebook. Where schools do get into trouble is by poking around in student Facebook pages.

This is where the Horace Mann School erred. Adam Kenner, Horace Mann's technology director, had demonstrated to teachers how to monitor student Facebook pages with a Horace Mann e-mail account, a false name, and a year of graduation. One intrepid teacher followed these instructions and stumbled upon a flood of Facebook pages that attacked teachers and mocked student clubs with vile, offensive language. The situation exploded in the hands of Horace Mann's head of school Thomas Kelly. The key question centered on who writes the rules of use regarding Facebook and how or if schools should get involved. Horace Mann discovered that if a school pokes around in student Facebook pages, there will be a lawsuit waiting. Parents of the Horace Mann students sued the school for violating the privacy of their children. In *New York* magazine (March 30, 2008), one of the parents who sued is quoted: "What you [the school] did was like breaking into my daughter's room and reading her diary."

However, if and when parents or other students send the school screenshots of walls, chats, and postings that cross the lines of propriety (of course, this is the ultimate test—what is offensive to one person, especially an adult, may be seen as perfectly innocuous by a student), then the school simply cannot ignore the call for help or intervention.

How the school intervenes is critical. Approaching the student in question from a punitive perspective drives a deep wedge between the student and the school. Instead, educators need to handle students with respect, care, and concern. They need to explain to students that what ends up on their Facebook wall can live forever and, increasingly, can stay with them as they apply to high school and college. More and more admissions officers are trolling Facebook to learn more about their applicants. Employers have been doing this for some time as well. Also, inviting parents into the dialogue with students opens the possibility for communication at home. Many parents have no clue what Facebook is all about; having the school act as intermediary allows them to learn about Facebook and take a more active role in educating their children about online behavior.

Many teachers friend their students, though some draw clear boundaries and only friend students who have graduated. This is an issue schools need to address with their faculty. Students often do not use the privacy settings on Facebook largely because they have not taken the time to learn how or because they honestly do not care that the whole world can see their photos and comments. Teachers can often step in and help students with whom they are friends on Facebook and encourage them to use the privacy settings.

However, student–teacher interaction on Facebook is a slippery slope, and it is wise for schools to take time to talk through the many challenges that these friendships can bring. Teachers sometimes do not think before they post, and students can then gain access that is not appropriate to a part of their teacher's life. This is the extreme case but one that can happen.

Parents want to know where schools stand. One parent wrote: "What are the appropriate communications between teacher and student?" Teachers can sometimes lose sight of boundaries and act without thinking in their online communications with students. Schools would be remiss not to address these situations with faculty. In one case, a teacher was found to be instant messaging with a student at 2:30 a.m. The parents were understandably concerned, and the only reason they knew about this was because they had open access to their child's AOL Instant Messenger account. They approached their son, and he admitted to the time and discussion, but the content of the exchange was related to a school project. It was more the time of the exchange that alarmed the parents. Still, one has to wonder how and why their son had computer access at such a late hour and why the teacher chose to respond with an instant message at that hour.

I realized that I needed to do a better job in my role as an administrator of articulating clear guidelines to teachers, so the lines could not be so easily blurred. One change that we immediately put in place was to have teachers communicate with students and families using their school e-mail account instead of a personal Gmail or Yahoo account. We still have not landed on a policy regarding contact with students on Facebook, though we are beginning those conversations.

Some teachers keep their Facebook pages closed and bound from intrusion by colleagues, students, and parents. They want to preserve their privacy. One faculty member shared that she politely declines friend requests from her colleagues. She lets them know that she appreciates the invitation but that she wants to keep her work life separate from her personal life. However, she did say that she feels funny when she then sees the colleague the next day at school. The online rejection can create social awkwardness in real time.

The more school communities can be open about Facebook, the healthier relationships among students, teachers, and parents will be. Invite experts on cyberbullying to school to disclose the realities to students, to signal to students that the school cares, and to let students know that if they are being bullied, they should seek out an adult in the community to help them. Parent evenings, where conversations are held about challenges parents face in trying to legislate their child's screen time, can often yield wonderful results, most significantly in reassuring parents that they are not alone and that the school community can work together to make sense of social networking.

The ultimate goal is for parents to know how to help their children when things go awry. Smart parenting means putting the computer in an open space at home, in full view, so that parents can step in and help. One parent shares her strategy regarding laptop location:

> We have our kids use their computers in the kitchen, so I can help anyone who needs it. It helps me keep an eye on the content of the sites they are visiting ("That site doesn't look very appropriate; let's see where else we can find information on that subject.") and also on whether they are staying focused.

The last thing parents should do is tune out or assume everything is okay. And, parents need to know that schools are there to help them make sense of what can be the tumultuous world of Facebook.

It took our school until the beginning of the third year of the 1-to-1 laptop program to move away from fear and move toward Facebook or opportunity, hope, and possibility with parents. After a parent education morning with Alan November, there was a palpable sense of excitement at news of engagement with children that did not harp on fear. Instead, the message was for parents to be present with their children with technology. One parent captures this seismic shift in thinking:

> Thank you for sponsoring Alan November to talk to us parents. He gave me hope and inspiration as a parent to accept the technologies and ensuing information, and to not be afraid but pay attention to the teachable moments. Just this yesterday, to mitigate my constant worrying, I resolved that something "bad" will happen to my son—but now "bad" has turned into a teachable moment. I needed this reminder.

chapter 6

privacy
and Little Brother

Finding the balance between appropriate oversight
and students' rights and needs for privacy is
anything but easy. Understanding that students will
attempt to and often succeed in overcoming security
measures makes it critical for you to get their buy-in.
Students need to understand the rules and why
they are in place, and schools need to channel their
energies productively.

A t the start of Cory Doctorow's 2008 teen techno-geek rebellion novel, *Little Brother*, the main character, Marcus Yallow,
gets hauled into the principal's office for hacking into the school's
secure database to steal standardized tests. The principal, confident
of his "reliable intelligence" work, threatens to expel Marcus. In
defiance and even with a bit of arrogance, Marcus calls the principal's bluff and encourages him to contact the police and his parents.
This tactic throws the principal, who, frustrated and in a fury,
sends Marcus back to class. Marcus complies, and on his return to

class walks past "idiotic" gait-recognition cameras installed by the school as a security measure. A gait-recognition camera, Marcus informs us, is "a biometric identifier, like fingerprints or retina-scans." He's figured out how to bypass this security measure, too.

Marcus reenters "classroom mode" and unpacks his school-issued laptop. His school, he tells us, monitors network traffic and "every click, keeping track of every fleeting thought you put over the net." Marcus informs the reader that cracking the laptop restrictions was "easy" to do. It involved nothing more than a quick download of a DVD image and the installation of hidden programs on the machine, "programs that would stay hidden even when the Board of Ed did its daily remote integrity checks of the machines." Marcus continues to rant against the archaic web browser "that no one under the age of 40 used voluntarily." Of course, he has an alternate browser he uses.

The key message of the opening scene of Little Brother is how irretrievably advanced kids are with technology and how sadly far behind schools are. Doctorow's novel is available free online via Creative Commons (http://creativecommons.org), a site that allows readers to share, remix, and reuse content. In the introduction to his text, Doctorow invites readers to "use the ideas to spark important discussions with your friends and family."

Neal Gaiman, author of Anansi Boys, in an endorsement of Little Brother, blogs: "I'd recommend Little Brother over pretty much any book I've read this year, and I'd want to get it into the hands of as many smart 13-year-olds, male and female, as I can." He does not need to worry. At Nueva, the 1-to-1 laptop has given us a window into the Doctorow generation of savvy computer users, issues of privacy and monitoring, and ways to redirect students toward productive uses of technology.

Apple Remote Desktop (ARD) is one vehicle schools use to ensure proper computer use. Do schools have the right to monitor student computer use at school with a program like ARD? And, if so, what is the best way for schools to monitor students without inciting an all-out riot?

In one incident at Nueva, a teacher confiscated a laptop after the tech office verified, through ARD, that a student was playing an online multiplayer game called Runescape during class time. The tech office sent screen shots of the student's activity to my office, and the evidence was indisputable. Many teachers had previously shared concerns about this student's online activity during classes, and there was a clear behavioral pattern of transgression.

I ran into the student's mother after school, fortuitously, the same day that we learned of his gaming in class. She shared her challenges in monitoring her son's activity and admitted that she does not have him use his computer in a public space at home. "I am overwhelmed, and the school gave him this machine, and I don't know how to monitor him," she confided.

We strategized and arrived at the conclusion that her son would be asked to leave his laptop in my office during the school day, unless he needed it for a particular class, like writing, for example. I also encouraged her to have him power down each night no later than 9 p.m. and suggested that she keep the laptop in her bedroom through the night. She agreed to this approach. Her son almost immediately began to demonstrate greater responsibility and restraint in his computer use at school. She also reported a better home environment because she could point to the school's suggestions to power down at 9 p.m. and to take the laptop from him.

Another parent expressed frustration over her inability to regulate her son's computer activity at home:

> When he has homework time, unless I am actually looking at his computer screen to make sure he is working on homework, he is either IMing or playing an Internet war game. This is a very frustrating and concerning situation for me as a parent. My son is required by Nueva to use a

computer for almost all schoolwork, yet I am not given the tools to monitor his use effectively. At home, much of his computer time for schoolwork is spent off task. I wonder how much of this happens at school?

This same parent raises important concerns about schools and monitoring, highlighting the efforts and responsibility that are necessary to provide a safe, balanced learning environment:

I received notice today from a teacher that my son was caught playing Urban Terror at recess. I am deeply troubled about this on a number of levels. The first is that my son was interacting with a computer rather than going out for recess to play and run and jump. The second is the extremely violent nature of the game, which seems to nurture all the things that parents dread for their children. The third is that, even though my son knows he is forbidden to play this kind of game, at school he was able to play it. I am so glad he was caught by one of the teachers, and this is certainly an excellent example of the Nueva staff's awareness of computer-related problems and their vigilant attempts to monitor students. Ideally, my son would be mature enough to know what is appropriate and when because it is impossible to expect that Nueva staff will be able to monitor him at all times. However, since my son is 11, it's not reasonable to expect that he will always or even often choose to do the right thing when temptation is frequently sitting in view, beckoning ...

I'd like to ask for your help with this problem. How can I feel reasonably sure that my son is safely and appropriately using his computer when he's at school? How can I be sure that he isn't opting to use the computer during free time when he should be outside expending his abundant physical energies? This is a problem that has the potential to do damage to my son—if only because of the opportunity costs. How can I protect him?

The school took several steps with this particular student. He had to use a loaner computer in place of his school-issued laptop. He was also monitored during classes through ARD, and his parents were made aware that this was taking place. At home, his parents imposed restrictions concerning where he could use the laptop and at what time each night he had to power down. Also, the parents confiscated his laptop and kept it in their bedroom during the night, as they were worried that he would sneak out of his room to use the laptop if it were left in a common family space.

Fortunately, this student gravitated toward video art and enrolled in a "Space Arts" elective to design, create, produce, and distribute a video, using his school-issued laptop. The class allowed students to explore and innovate with the crossover between the worlds of arts and sciences. Students engaged in exercises relating to Zero Gravity arts (such as using the Star Dome and creating science fiction animations) and then explored creating planetary textures using plaster and other materials. As a culmination, students created a zero gravity art project for a future parabolic flight. In tandem with another classmate, this particular student built two circular disks, spray painted them purple, green, and silver and attached strings to the tops of the disks so that they could hang from ceilings and walls to simulate extraterrestrial beings as seen by humans for the first time. After his father viewed the film at an Arts presentation, he commented: "Now that's a good use of those laptops. My son was engaged in a productive project, and he had to use the laptop for learning and creativity." Also, his son's energies were redirected from distraction and transgression to a meaningful learning experience.

Some teachers actually welcome the use of ARD as an antidote to classroom discipline. Teachers do not want students off task, playing games, or looking at inappropriate websites in class. They feel like they are on an island, and with ARD, they know they have a safeguard. Even so, they feel uncomfortable about asking the tech office to monitor class activity. One teacher remarked:

It's a damned if you do, damned if you don't situation. If you do monitor with ARD, students grow resentful, and trust is lost in the classroom. But if you don't, and students play games or flip screens to hide their activity, then trust is lost also. I want to know what's happening in my classroom, and I want to follow-up with students and their parents. The last thing I want is for students to "get away" with off-task behavior.

One tech administrator shared his approach to using ARD. He periodically checks activity in high-volume classrooms, and if he sees students playing games or surfing off-topic websites, he alerts the classroom teacher to what is going on. He does not make a big deal about it, but if there is a pattern of transgression, he follows up with the student and student's family.

In students' minds, though, being monitored in this way evokes a picture of a room filled with computer monitors tracking every second of their online behavior. "It is an Orwellian nightmare for students," one teacher commented.

Students are naturally curious and want to explore the potential of computers. However, this can sometimes lead them into troubling situations, such as attempting to gain system administration ("root") access to other students' computers. In one situation, using ARD, our IT director discovered the following about a student's activity:

> There are repeated attempts by him to try to gain access (via SSH) [Secure Shell network protocol] to other students' computers. There is also history showing that he made direct connections to our mail server through the Unix shell. Doing this would let him send faked e-mails from someone else without leaving a trace on his own computer (or our server). We cannot know with certainty that he sent those messages (or any); we can only know with certainty that he connected to the server in this non-standard, untraceable way. We looked at the terminal

logs. We were able to do this remotely, without student knowledge. He also has made these back-door connections to our mail server and also appears to have hacked the administrative access to his computer and established root access to his computer.

When we confronted the student, we asked him why he had done this. His response: "I was curious and wanted to see if I could do it, and I could. I thought it was funny to spoof e-mails." It was clear that the motivation to bypass school measures to keep the community secure drove this student's actions. As we discussed the situation, we learned of his passion for programming, and he shared that he wished the school offered a programming class.

So, at the beginning of year two, we offered a programming elective to our seventh and eighth graders, and it was overwhelmingly subscribed to by students who had been involved in hacking administrator passwords. They needed a productive outlet for their curiosity and budding hacker skills. The class was an introduction to creating database-enabled websites using MySQL (a relational database management system) and PHP (a general purpose scripting language). Students looked at the fundamental principles of relational database design. They also created dynamic websites to read and write data back to the database.

Projects varied. One student created a website that allowed students to bring snacks for Advisory class, and the most critical lesson the student learned was the importance of the back-end database to support the front-end website seen by viewers. Another student developed a restricted-access website where users could log in and play various games.

Instead of steering their energies toward cracking the administrator password, these students now devoted hours inside and outside of class to devising websites that they and their community could use for both entertainment and practical purposes.

We began to notice a marked change in student behavior and attitudes toward the laptop program and toward technology at school. One student remarked to the IT director: "I had no idea how much work it takes to maintain the back end of a website." Also, in year two, we had no instances of students cracking the administrator password. It could be that students just grew more savvy and sophisticated in their ability to bypass security, but we like to think that the shift in our thinking toward educating and bringing students into finding practical solutions helped to turn the tide away from breaking trust and toward working with and cultivating community. It was the tidal shift from fear to Facebook.

Beyond using ARD to regulate and monitor student behavior, it is important that teachers know they are protected from student transgressions in the classroom. One educator who visits many different schools says that when he comes to a new school, the first thing he does is ask students which proxy they use to bypass the school filters. Students are not shy about sharing this information and freely offer full disclosure. When he asks the students why they think schools have the filters, students often respond, "It's to protect the teachers."

In one incident at Nueva, a student encouraged another student to go to an objectionable site during a class. Fortunately, the school filters blocked access. However, the student was naturally curious to see the site, so he went home and opened it because his home did not have filters and he could access the material. He told his mother a slightly different version of the story, that he had left his computer to go to the bathroom and another student in the class had opened the site, and when he returned to sit down, the screen displayed the objectionable content.

What the son neglected to share was that he had accessed the site at home, not at school. In my conversation with the teacher, I learned that the teacher had not witnessed any inappropriate activity during the class itself.

I informed the parent of the steps we take to ensure student safety and security:

> Nueva blocks several web portals for obvious reasons, and the tech staff can review these with you if you would like. Tech checked the web filtering on campus, and that site is blocked and is inaccessible from campus. According to students involved, the only image that appeared on the screen was the web filter signal saying access was denied. Again, according to the other students involved, your son did not leave the classroom and did not leave his computer unattended. He was told by another student to type in that website, and he did type it into his computer but was unable to access it. We reviewed your son's computer today to look at his history, but he had erased the history.

These are challenging issues for schools to handle, but the benefit of having filters is that it does help to give teachers peace of mind to know that students cannot access inappropriate material while they are in class. However, with all that we have learned about the ease with which students can skirt school filters, it is difficult to know if we ever landed on the truth in the situation just mentioned. We did due diligence to investigate the student's computer to see what sites he had accessed, but the student had emptied his browser search history, so we were unable to know for sure what had happened. The bottom line in this situation is that the student ended up quite embarrassed about having seen the pornographic images, and the parents grew more comfortable in their knowledge that the school had taken steps to provide a safe learning environment.

Parents themselves sometimes are less than forthcoming about all of the information involved in cases of Internet malfeasance. I received a phone call from a parent concerned about the instant messaging going on between her child and another child. She came in to meet with me to share a printed copy of a heated, profanity-laden instant message (IM) exchange between her child and another student. I read the exchange and concurred with her worries. I then brought in the other set of parents. They brought in a printed copy of the IM transcript as well, but their copy read quite differently from the initial copy I received. The first parent had edited out certain language her son had used, but she neglected to let me know that she had done so. I went back to the first parent and asked what had happened. Quite embarrassed, she admitted to removing her son's language from her printed copy. This is the tripwire for schools. It is so easy to manipulate and fabricate what transpires on the Internet, and it can be difficult for schools to successfully and completely unearth what students (and parents) are actually doing.

Schools must be watchful to tread wisely and carefully when approaching issues of privacy and the Internet with students and families. In addition, schools need to seek out ways to proactively engage students in meaningful learning experiences, such as programming or video space art, to inspire and redirect students away from unnecessary distractions. The key is to steer students toward opportunities for responsible online and computer behavior. The more that sort of instruction is embedded in technology, the easier it will be for school communities to instill grounded ethical behavior in students.

But the fear of the loss of privacy, a concern strongly associated with the use of certain types of online programs and sharing, can present significant hurdles to teachers who are eager to utilize the latest tools to engage students in learning. For example, one innovative teacher was eager to initiate an exchange with a school in Singapore. Her plan was to use discussion boards to that end. She suggested the use of one created on her teacher home page inside of the Nueva secure website, but the school in Singapore was concerned with this. They wanted to use a password-protected discussion forum not associated with either school, so both sets of students could access and view the discussions in the future if they wanted to. However, for reasons of security and safety, the Nueva School does not place student information on external websites. What began as an inspired attempt to globalize learning soon ran into roadblocks around privacy, access, and the risk of opening both communities to the unfiltered world of the Internet. The teacher devised a different solution. She decided to have the discussions via e-mail, and the students copied the teachers on all messages they sent.

This same teacher set up a customized search engine on Google, one that allows teachers to build a list of relevant, critical content-based websites, and her goals were quite clear:

> In terms of the Google site, my intention there is not to filter information based on the message. My intention is to remove inappropriate material based on the "reasonable parent" standard. While our firewall here at Nueva is pretty thorough, it does not always block everything. For example, last year I had my fifth grade students researching various elements of the Ancestral Puebloan people. Some students chose to research the weapons used by the Anasazi. They often came across websites with inappropriate images or content that was missed by our firewall. By choosing a plethora of appropriate websites in advance and placing them on my personalized Google site, I was able to make sure the students got the information they needed without being exposed to imagery that was not appropriate in a school. Likewise, I had the same group do a project relating to maritime archeology, focusing on sunken pirate ships. I'm sure you can guess how many websites are out there about pirates that really don't have any educational content or relative information regarding the assignment. The kids even found quite a few online pirate games. So, by searching out the sites that had information relevant to the project at hand in advance, I helped the students focus and avoid getting distracted by some pretty cool, but irrelevant websites. Because computer use on campus is limited to educational purposes only, I think it is helpful to the students and classroom time management to limit the vast world of the Internet down to a

more useful and relevant search base. Their computers at home can be used, in conjunction with parental guidance and education, for searches unrelated to classroom goals and assignments.

Here is teaching with technology at its best. A thoughtful, seasoned teacher harnessed a technology tool to enhance teaching and learning and to play the role of the adult in guiding students toward smart, safe searching, grounded in the course content.

Privacy is a double-edged sword for schools and teachers. It is critical to preserve and guarantee a safe learning environment, but it is also harder and harder to maintain, given the free, open access world of the Internet. And, teachers are looking to tap the free online tools to make learning more authentic, collaborative, and meaningful for students. One teacher wanted to use Google Docs in her classroom for online journaling. She created a document for each student and then wanted to give access to the parents, to allow both students and parents to respond to online journaling prompts. She recognized that "in theory" the site would be secure because she had limited the access to relevant persons. She also had thought through privacy concerns and was ready to review them with students and parents. However, again, because Google Docs is an external site, Nueva did not allow her to do this. Instead, the school devised a way for her to accomplish the same objectives of collaboration and feedback on the secure school website by creating a blog for each student and family. In this instance, there was a clear, secure alternative, the teacher's energies were easily redirected, and the learning objectives were accomplished.

When it comes to the issue of privacy online in schools, there are several options available that constructively reorient teaching and learning while remaining sensitive to the concerns of communities wishing to safeguard children from inappropriate content, in the form of games or websites filled with objectionable content. It is a delicate balancing act, and the pendulum can easily swing toward fear and shut down opportunities for innovation and exploration of new tools and strategies to engage students in learning. It is critical to hold students accountable and to let them know that someone is watching out for their well-being online. At the same time, it is essential that schools provide outlets for students to experiment in a safe environment in the form of programming or space art.

The bottom line is that schools need to listen to students to hear their concerns, passions, and interests and then develop programs to meet these needs. If schools do not provide this opportunity for students to be heard, they run the risk of student disengagement and an endless game of cat and mouse, in which administrators' energies will be wasted trying to control such student transgressions as hacking administrator passwords or spoofing e-mail accounts. With teachers, schools need to remind themselves that teachers want to innovate and develop exciting curricula with the latest tools, and if schools introduce teachers to these tools, they have to expect that teachers will want to use them with students. When such conflicts arise, there are often options available within a secure school website that can help teachers accomplish their learning objectives with students.

Schools need to devote time and energy to finding curricular solutions that can embed technology when the situation calls for it. School administrators are constantly in the position of steering forward progress and making sure that the community stays on the right track. Every day there are judgment calls. The hope is that school officials will take the time to think through all the issues in a given situation to ensure that students are both protected and challenged to learn in new and interesting ways with technology.

Schools face the challenge of creating safe learning environments for students while fostering innovative, forward-thinking curriculum development with technology. It is easy to get stuck like the squirrel on a slippery slope when addressing these goals, and schools' efforts can easily be foiled, as described in Little Brother, where students like Marcus Yallow seize the upper hand. Schools can set reasonable parameters without creating oppressive atmospheres that invite student rebellion. Open communication among students, teachers, administrators, and parents helps ensure buy-in for necessary security measures.

chapter 7

teacher development
A Field of Dreams?

Although students often grasp technology almost instinctively, most teachers need time and training in order to effectively integrate technology into their teaching styles and goals.

In the 1989 movie *Field of Dreams*, Iowa farmer Ray Kinsella follows a voice in his cornfield that instructs him, "If you build it, he will come." He reads this message as an edict to build a baseball field on his farm, where the ghosts of "Shoeless" Joe Jackson and the other seven Chicago White Sox players banned from the game for throwing the 1919 World Series magically appear. Ray pours all of his energies into the building project, against a rising tide of opposition, because he is a dreamer and a visionary and maybe even a little half-baked. School administrators and tech directors need to be careful to avoid the trappings of a *Field of Dreams* model toward changing teaching and learning with the latest gadgetry. One school web developer explained:

We have more technology than 95% of the faculty use already. This may be an education issue, an edict issue, a "they-don't-want-it" issue, or a "it's not exactly what we need" issue (or a combination of all of the above). My suspicion is that the teaching methods here don't readily make use of online stuff. We have to do some work beforehand to find out what it is the faculty needs instead of trying a "field of dreams" model (e.g., if we build it, will they use it?).

Two years later, this same web developer shared that teachers had started to really leverage and use the system he developed using online discussion forums, wikis, and blogs on the Nueva School website. However, as a result, he needed to go back and rewire and fix "bugs" that surfaced from the heavy amount of use the teachers were putting on the system. In his words, "This is a good problem for me to have—at least the teachers are now using it."

One very inspired classroom teacher who attended Alan November's "Building Learning Communities" summer conference in Boston generated the interest and spread of the use of wikis. She returned from the experience completely energized and open to exploring all of the different tools the school website offers. She writes of her experience with November:

I was so incredibly inspired by Alan November's "Building Learning Communities" conference using technology in education. I began by creating a class wiki where we could share all of the new projects with which we would be experimenting throughout the year. Wiki means quick. It's a Hawaiian word. Participants can make an original content contribution or modify content that is already there. Teachers can start wikis and seed them with problems, questions, ideas, and content from the class. Students can respond, solve problems, post their work, and respond to their classmates. It seems like a simple idea, but the more I thought about it the more I realized that it could be far more than a collection of tech projects—it could be a way to completely change the entire curriculum.

Her excitement was infectious and spread fast to other teachers, and before we knew it, we had a wiki/blog/discussion forum epidemic on our hands. Middle and lower school teachers were very excited by the possibilities of extending the classroom beyond the school day at home and into the evening hours.

The widespread use of these tools did not come without problems, however. Teachers were still new to the tools and did not completely understand or anticipate the problems that could arise with the proliferation of posting, uploading, and sharing. For example, one student had posted on the class wiki a video she made using Jing, which allows users to capture anything on their computer screen and share it instantly as an image or short movie. This student's work disappeared from the wiki. She was naturally upset after the hard work she had put into the project. Several other students had the same thing happen. Our director of technology needed to send out a primer to the teachers on how to use and edit a wiki as opposed to a blog. In the primer, he explained:

A wiki page is editable by everyone in a group, so there is no bypassing of the system. These wiki pages are different than the blog pages commonly seen on the Nueva website. A wiki page is designed to allow a group of authorized users to make edits to the entire page. A wiki page is highly collaborative by design, and is based on a level of trust—trust that people would respect the content enough not to remove it. Even when honoring mutual respect, it is still possible to unintentionally and accidentally overwrite someone else's content. This happens when there are simultaneous saves to the same page.

In another classroom, a teacher wondered how to more fully engage all students in discussion and was introduced, in the organic fashion that a culture of innovation brings, to an online, time-controlled chat program called TodaysMeet. This program, according to its website, "helps you embrace the backchannel and connect with your audience in realtime." TodaysMeet asks users to "encourage the room to use the live stream to make comments, ask questions, and use that feedback to tailor your presentation, sharpen your points, and address audience needs" (TodaysMeet.com). This teacher jumped right into using the program, and students loved it. Discussions took on a whole new life, with many of the quieter students now contributing ideas and questions. However, one of the unintended consequences was the creation of backchannels behind the backchannel. "The backchannel," according to the TodaysMeet website, "is everything going on in the room that isn't coming from the presenter." In the Nueva classroom, students started to create their own chat rooms behind the class discussion taking place, and many of their comments were off topic and even inappropriate. When I asked the teacher about this, he said that he was not surprised, and he even expected that to happen. He brought the class together to create norms around appropriate use and to agree to stay on task during the "Meet." The first time he used the program, he told the kids to just "go" and "play," and then he stopped the students and had them debrief how the tool worked and what the trouble spots were.

This teacher started to invite me to his classes through TodaysMeet. This helps to keep me plugged into what is happening in the classroom with technology and learning. In this classroom environment, the students are allowed to run with the technology tool—but only with the guidance of a thoughtful teacher who knows how to ask the right questions and how to steer students toward maximizing a technology tool for learning.

This is a key point. Technology in the hands of seasoned teachers is critical. My wife is a first grade teacher with 17 years of teaching experience, and she has undergone a dramatic transformation in her teaching with technology since we made the move to California from New Jersey. She now regularly uses iWork's Keynote presentation software (which is similar to PowerPoint) and Pages (a word processing and page layout application) for student projects, parent communication, and documentation of the learning process. A year ago, she did not use any of these programs (or their PC equivalents). However, her partnership with a teaching associate in her mid-twenties, who was versed in and fluent with various applications, helped to kick-start her move toward greater technology integration. My wife knows the content of her teaching practice, and she will think through a teaching topic with her teaching associate, who then helps to imagine different ways to utilize and integrate technology. As my wife explained:

> I talk through lesson ideas with her, and she then maps out the technology to match the goals of the lesson. Using technology in the classroom is a lot like teaching writing. It is all about knowing your audience. For example, Pages works beautifully for my parent newsletter. I have a template, and I add photos and text. My teaching associate created the template, and then she taught me how to play with the form.

Also, her school has a comprehensive initiative to move in a more ecofriendly direction, so every project she considers in her teaching forces her to think about how sustainable the outcome will be. For example, instead of creating and laminating posters to hang up, she deploys Keynote to run on her Smart Board in the classroom. "Why would I cut up all of that paper and cover it in plastic," she asks, "when I can use Keynote to accomplish the same goal and it is easier to keep a copy for next year?" In addition, one of her teaching goals for the year was to use technology more effectively:

> It's a lot easier to focus on technology at this point in my career, at year 16, because I have achieved mastery in other areas, like the teaching of reading, writing, and math. Of course, I still have work to do in those areas, but I am pretty far along in my pedagogy. With technology, I have to give greater energy and focus, and I can do that because it's one major area of growth for me instead of four.

Interestingly, at her New Jersey school, she had two computers in her classroom, but "all the kids did was play educational games," she commented. Also, students were dropped off at the computer lab for their tech classes, and she could use the "free" period for planning. At her current school, there is no computer lab. Instead, the tech teacher brings the laptop cart to her classroom, and she co-plans lessons that are integrated into the curriculum. She can't escape, as she could at her New Jersey school. The technology class time is a vital part of her teaching schedule, as important and integral as reading, writing, and math. The more time she spends sitting next to her first grade students, the more she sees how to use the technology within the context of a social studies unit, for example. In addition, her students are patient with her when she asks for their help in understanding how to use an application. She has no qualms about being the student next to a 6-year-old teacher: "It's healthy to flip roles with my students. It constantly reminds me how they feel each day in school when they have to learn new things."

At one of her school's faculty meetings, the technology teacher highlighted my wife's use of Pages for her newsletter and showed a completed newsletter to the staff. One teacher asked, with a combination of fear and awe, "Are we all going to have to start doing that?" The problem with sharing technology exemplars with other teachers is that it can cause more anxiety than excitement about possibilities. For many teachers, technology feels like an "add-on" and is intimidating even to think about.

At Nueva, we organized a series of teacher-led technology workshops in year one of the laptop program. The goal was to create the chance for master teachers to present their use of technology in the context of their teaching, so as to inspire the rest of the faculty. The school's web developer echoed the overarching premise behind the workshops:

> Seriously though, I do know that unless the faculty becomes fluent in the technology, it will never be an

effective teaching tool—independently of whether or not it should be an effective teaching tool.

The question is, what is the best way for faculty to gain technological fluency without spoiling the efforts of the web developers who are constantly shifting and realigning the focus of their efforts to give faculty the tools to enhance teaching and learning? Again, in the words of the school's web developer:

> My experience to date has been that faculty rarely, with a few exceptions, think out of the box and make suggestions. So I'm not sure where we end up: we can build this stuff, but do the faculty and students really want it, and do they have the time and desire to use it?

These are very real and valid concerns. He continues his thinking:

> It is not unlike the diet book craze. If people acted rationally, there would be one diet book in the world because they all basically tell us to eat less and exercise more. But since people fail at that, they think, "Oh this new catchy title will fix all my weight problems" and they buy a new book. Technology operates the same way. If blogs and e-mail don't seem to work, then RSS feeds and Ning will solve all our problems, when in fact they won't

The teacher-led workshops hit broadly on a variety of applications, such as Keynote and Electronic Mindmapping, and motivated teachers to learn more but also crystallized how much work they still had to do. In addition, the workshops occurred out of context, even though the workshop leaders shared how they incorporated applications into the curriculum. Given the amount of effort that went into preparing the workshops, there was little direct or indirect yield, other than a feeling of inadequacy among many of the teachers.

One longtime Nueva tech educator urged patience in dealing with faculty development:

You need to allow for organic growth, teacher to teacher. The most effective and lasting way for teaching to change is when one teacher shares with another, grows inspired, and experiments with a new application. Force-feeding technology through workshops can sometimes backfire and actually slow growth.

However, two years later, we ran a similar round of teacher-led technology workshops and found a vastly different result. There was an organic feeling to the workshops, and instead of having teachers rotate through two workshops in 90 minutes, we settled on one 90-minute workshop. This time the topics resonated more clearly with faculty. We offered workshops on iWork's Pages, Comic Life, the iLife Suite, the Live Scribe pen, and one on increasing the efficiency of online research with students.

In advance of the workshops, I used Pages to send communications to faculty, in which I shared this description of Pages from the iWork Pages website:

> Pages is both a streamlined word processor and an easy-to-use page layout tool. It allows you to be a writer one minute and a designer the next, always with a perfect document in the works.

I also prepared the workshop agenda using Pages. It generated a buzz before the meeting, and many teachers asked me how I was creating the documents. Many of them attended the workshop I ran on Pages. It took all of 20 minutes for me to teach them how to use the program, and we used the rest of the workshop time creating Pages documents related to class newsletters, curriculum summaries of the week, and invitations to class events. One fifth grade teacher immediately created her weekly newsletter to parents and sent it out a few days later. She says she will never look back. The response she received from parents was positive and reinforced for her the importance of being open to learning how to use new technology tools.

The second offering of the tech workshops yielded a more direct, positive, and lasting impact. One teacher commented:

It was much better this time. You gave us time to play, and you did not overload us with information. Also, we could all think of ways to immediately implement [Pages] into our weekly and daily planning.

The most dramatic example of a change in teacher behavior toward technology in the classroom at Nueva occurred with one of our longest-tenured faculty members. At the onset of the laptop program in 2007, at an October faculty meeting that dealt with technology in the classroom, this teacher stated that she would rather stick to pencil and paper instead of using laptops for learning. A year later, she completed a 180. Her course was online, she used blogs, she included links, she met with developers from CK–12, she invited experts to speak to her students about effective Internet research, and she took risks in front of her students, confident that she could learn but knowing that she did not have all of the skills at her fingertips.

When I asked her why and how she had changed her attitude toward technology, she explained:

I was stuck and I don't like to be stuck. I like to take risks and I could see the possibilities of the library of knowledge. For example, I looked up *Don Quixote* on Google Books and found an 1854 translation. That's just unbelievable.

She continued:

I can't deal with the hardware and I don't want to deal with the hardware. Let tech do that piece. I want to play with the software with kids. I like to change and grow. It's what keeps things interesting.

However, she also admitted to some discomfort about technology:

I don't like it. It's hard for me, but I'm going to do it and keep on doing it, and I'm at a school that prides itself on innovation and risk-taking, so I'll be okay.

She still likes to use her mini-notebook to keep track of her to-do lists, even though she owns an iPhone and could use the Notes application: "It's too much work to take out the phone, click on the application and then peck on the keypad to type in my notes," she states. But, as one of her students pointed out, she would use it if there were an easier-to-use version. And that's the reality of technology. There is always one more level to go to. She likes to joke with her husband, "Where is the antigravity machine?"

Her mantra with students is "Research is not a straight line." Another teacher, deeply embedded in the teaching of research skills to students, notes the challenges endemic to teaching research skills today:

> Although printed material is not necessarily accurate, there is a general belief that published materials have been vetted. The dynamic and open nature of the World Wide Web does not imply the same editorial review. With the mass proliferation of blogging, the lines have been blurred further, burdening the researcher. Students must discern trustworthiness, weigh sources against each other, and separate the scholarly wheat from the popular chaff.

She goes on to explain the tools she needs to be a better teacher:

> Depth, however, entails more directed follow-up after a first look. Deepening research means more than clicking the links from one Wikipedia article to another. To research objectively and accurately, teachers need to urge students to consult published works from several sources, both online and printed. The teacher's role is still to teach critical thinking, but there's a whole heck of a lot more information out there to distill.

While teachers take stock of their own abilities to digest the prolific volume of information at their fingertips, one click of a button away, they also have to figure out ways to make meaning for students. It is a two-step process, and teachers are all over the map in their attitude toward tackling the technology. Schools do need to clear the obstacles that can impede teacher progress. Slow servers, small bandwidth, printer failures, and projector malfunctions can torture teachers and turn them against technology. "I don't want to have to deal with hardware issues. I just want to click one button and go," one teacher stated.

When my wife's school switched to a new website, she was left to fend for herself in transferring data to the new site. As she already juggles lesson planning, parent phone calls, and devoting attention to her students, she could not believe that the school could not manage this process for her. This is exactly the kind of bureaucratic mangling that can doom teacher attitudes toward technology. It felt like one more thing to do instead of being an integral part of her work as a teacher.

Teachers are at school to teach students, and schools cannot lose sight of this fundamental aspect of education, even as they transition to new technologies and infrastructures. Teacher development is a field of dreams, matched only by the ability of schools to streamline systems management with vision and professional development for teachers.

One effective way to transform teachers with technology is to devise and implement a comprehensive teacher evaluation system, with multiple visits to classrooms by a team of colleagues and principals. The teams observe the teacher at work but also gauge the level of student engagement and learning through the course of a lesson or unit of study. The teacher's ability to motivate and construct meaningful learning through careful questioning instead becomes the metric by which teachers are judged in their ability to bolster student achievement. Comprehensive teacher evaluation programs can also act as a perfect pivot point for encouraging teachers to reorient teaching practice with technology and to place a greater emphasis on customization. Evaluations not only give schools an opportunity to critique the current practices of teachers but also can direct teachers' transition toward technology. However, this cannot happen without professional development plans, administrative and institutional support, and a clear vision of the utility of technology to promote, advance, and customize learning for students.

Another benefit gained from teacher evaluation teams composed of colleagues is that teachers have the opportunity to pick up tricks of the trade when they observe their colleagues in action. During one observation, a teacher used Comic Life, a program that allows users to create authentic comics. This teacher incorporated Comic Life into a unit on Greek myths and had students develop comic strips about different mythical figures, from Athena to Zeus. One of the observing teachers had never seen this application in action. She was so excited to learn about it that she immediately incorporated it into her unit on Native American myths the next day. And, her colleague provided instructions for her to use with her class to make the lesson run more fluidly. This is one subtle way to move teachers forward with technology.

Without support and coaching from a colleague, though, technology can act as a major stumbling block for learning. Malcolm Gladwell, writing in The New Yorker (December 15, 2008), shares an anecdote to illustrate a teacher rattled by what should be a simple, straightforward action of turning on a computer to share a PowerPoint presentation:

> Another teacher walked over to a computer to do a PowerPoint presentation, only to realize that she hadn't turned it on. As she waited for it to boot up, the classroom slid into chaos.

This is, of course, the greatest fear that technophobic teachers have. I can still recall my own early days in the classroom, trying to wrestle with cords and wires to plug in the LCD projector. I was grateful to have the help of a more skilled teacher, with whom I shared a classroom and who utilized technology more regularly than I did. He knew how to accomplish basic set-up and demonstrated the patience of Job in walking me through the steps to make the projector work for PowerPoint slides. This is not an insignificant hurdle for schools to clear when considering teacher development with technology.

"It stands to reason that to be a great teacher you have to have withitness," writes Gladwell (The New Yorker, 2008). Gladwell quotes educational researcher Jacob Kounin on effective teaching, which Kounin defines as "withitness":

> Withitness ... a teacher's communicating to the children by her actual behavior (rather than by verbally announcing: "I know what's going on") that she knows what the children are doing, or has the proverbial "eyes in the back of her head."

Schools need to find ways to instill "withitness" in teachers when they are using technology in the classroom. Technology "withitness" goes far beyond turning on the computer. It takes a master teacher, like my wife, to begin to know how to conceptualize meaningful curriculum. She already has "withitness" as a teacher, but schools need to provide structures, through appropriate assistant teacher partnerships and teacher evaluation programs, for example, to promote an environment of risk-taking and successful implementation of technology in the classroom.

November has commented on the importance of working with teachers and is a firm believer that "how to dismember media to teach content is the way to save democracy." However, school change with technology cannot happen in a piecemeal fashion. There needs to be a systematic, institutional embrace of technology as a tool to enhance teaching and learning. At Nueva, at the start of the laptop program in 2007, this critical organizational, conceptual, visionary element was lacking, and teachers and students floated under a rudderless 1-to-1 program. But, the speed with which the school seized the opportunity to educate teachers, parents, and administrators catapulted the community forward, and the culture of the school around technology changed completely.

Over a three-year period, laptop learning and teacher development grew exponentially. A combination of factors converged to make this growth possible. The school reached out to experts in the field, like Alan November, and invested time and money to bring him to campus to introduce teachers to the imaginative possibilities that technology offers. Also, the school sent a team of teachers to November's "Building Learning Communities" conference, and out of that experience teachers returned to campus energized and excited to share their new thinking and technical expertise with their colleagues. And, the school made the time to continue technology education during staff meeting time, revising our approach to meet the needs and interests of our faculty. Beyond these tangible measures, though, a spirit of technology innovation took hold. Small groups of teachers began to lead and introduce other teachers to technology tools, and teachers felt comfortable experimenting, knowing that they could draw on their colleagues for support and inspiration. In addition to the organic development of innovation and planning among teachers, the school also leveraged the expertise of its web developer to keep pace with the tools teachers were using, so that teachers could experiment in a seamless manner and not hit roadblocks that would thwart their forward progress.

Teacher development is a field of dreams, and if a school invests in the infrastructure and training and allows for "play" among the teachers, technology will enhance teaching and learning.

chapter 8

students and **laptops**
Making a Difference?

Undoubtedly, we learned an awful lot of valuable lessons as teachers and administrators during the first two years of the program. However, the priority has always been improving teaching and learning for the students. Have we made progress, and how is that measured?

Remarkably, year two of our laptop program ended with a whimper. Students turned in their laptops for summer repair, maintenance, and cleaning, and the process ran smoothly and without incident. At the end of year one, we had had to literally pry the laptops away from some students and their parents. Now, several students commented that they looked forward to the summer without the laptop, so that they could just "be outside and play." The temptation to hop on the laptop and play a game or e-mail or chat was too great for many students to manage, and they started to demonstrate greater understanding of themselves.

This is not easy to do, especially in a culture where it has become routine at corporate and business meetings to "Mind Your BlackBerry" instead of minding your manners. Alex Williams of the *New York Times* (June 21, 2009) quoted Philippe Reines (senior advisor to Hillary Clinton): "You'll have half the participants BlackBerrying each other as a submeeting, with a running commentary on the primary meeting. BlackBerrys have become like cartoon thought bubbles." The same article quoted David Brotherton (a media consultant in Seattle): [Bringing smartphones to meetings indicates] "I'm connected. I'm busy. I'm important. And if this meeting doesn't hold my interest, I've got 10 other things I can do instead."

Students in schools with laptops have the opportunity to learn firsthand how to balance etiquette with distraction.

Teachers and parents have to work very hard to mitigate the forces of distraction that inevitably accompany a 1-to-1 laptop program. One despairing mother reported that on the drive home from school, her son would jump in the car, open his laptop, and click away; at the same time, he would give a detailed account of the day's activities at school. When she asked him to stop using the laptop in the car, the student replied, "Why, Mom, I'm paying attention and talking to you." On one level, the student is not wrong. He sees himself being able to work on an application and have a conversation with the flow of both moving seamlessly. His mother, in contrast, feels slighted and disrespected. This is the delicate balance that schools, families, and students need to scale together.

One particularly eloquent eighth grade student articulated his growth over two years with the laptop program, stating:

> At the beginning of the seventh grade, I was given a laptop by my school and the responsibility to make good decisions. I was introduced to high tech ways of communicating, such as iChat and AIM. This was the first time that I had full access to technology. I wasn't used to being in full control of a computer. This resulted in me not

fully focusing on my studies, falling behind in school, because all I wanted to do when I got home was go on my computer, chatting with my friends on iChat, and playing video games. I was so focused on those games, and I really wanted to beat them really bad, and I had never experienced this obsession before. As the months went by, I started slipping in school, I was doing just enough to get by, and I didn't want to learn. My conference came along, and my dad confessed to my advisor, that he wasn't sure whether he wanted me to have a laptop, and that I was not at my full capacity when I wasn't focused on something. I realized that I did not need to focus on these video games, and I needed to focus on homework assignments. I turned around my school year, and got back on track. The rest of my school year, I think, was amazing. It made school that much more enjoyable, and I was learning that much more. I learned that when I am passionate about something, I really can go far. When I am focused in school, everything comes easy to me. I see that now, with my most recent commitments.

Things had gotten so bad for this particular student that his mother demanded that he leave the laptop at school at the end of each day. As he writes, he simply could not regulate his own behavior. What is particularly interesting about this student is that he is athletic and involved in a variety of extracurricular activities, from competitive basketball teams to musical drama. He is also a school leader. His peers listen to and respect his opinion. He is academically strong and participates eagerly in class discussions. But even for some of the best students, the laptop holds a certain irresistible pull, not unlike the compulsive smartphone behavior described in the New York Times BlackBerry article.

Another student reflected on her first year with the laptop. She writes:

The laptops take a lot of responsibility. You will have to learn to make sure you always know where your laptop is and you have to make sure it always has enough battery before you go to classes where your laptop is needed and you have to be SUPER careful that you do not drop it or damage it. Other than that, getting a new laptop is really cool because there are a ton of new applications you can explore.

This student recognizes the responsibility that comes with an expensive piece of equipment, but at the same she marvels at the world of applications that the laptop opens for her.

Another student expressed similar self-awareness:

When you are in class, don't play games with your laptop because you will be oblivious to what the teacher is telling you and you won't know what the homework is.

Schools fortunate enough to be able to fund a 1-to-1 laptop program would be remiss to pass up the lifelong learning opportunities that accompany such a program.

Technology can quickly become an appendage, and before we know it, we are playing computer games in class or texting friends and colleagues during meetings. Schools are an important laboratory for technology education of young people, not only in terms of technical proficiency, but also regarding basic etiquette and manners. Schools are fortunate to have opportunities to work with students at impressionable ages so that they can develop strategies for self-regulation. Otherwise, students will turn into prospective employees who sink their chances for success, like this young man described in the New York Times BlackBerry etiquette article:

In Dallas, a college student sunk his chance to have an internship at a hedge fund last summer when he pulled out a BlackBerry to look up a fact to help him make a point during his interview, then lingered—momentarily, but perceptibly—to check a text message a friend had sent, said Trevor Hanger, the head of equity trading at the hedge fund, who was helping conduct the interview. (Williams, 2009)

Alan November designs classrooms to unleash the forces of technology to engage in real-time, face-to-face dialogue and to allow for clicking away on a laptop. He assigns students different roles. One student is the note-taker, documenting in detail the topics being discussed. Another student is the big idea gatherer, capturing the main themes emerging in the discussion. And another student is the researcher, who digs into the web to uncover more information about the topic. Instead of combating online and web culture, November is creating ways to live productively within it. He rotates these jobs, and instead of cultivating an adversarial learning environment in which teachers must worry whether students are secretly playing video games, he finds ways to channel students' desire to interact with technology at school, thus insuring that they are connected to what is going on and that the computers more fully enhance classroom learning.

Beyond the classroom walls, though, schools need to attend to play culture. When schools introduce laptops, play at school takes on a different meaning. Students, particularly boys, start to disappear into the vortex of their computer screens and shirk opportunities for outdoor play. Online computer games begin to hold allure, and boys get caught up in the avatars of World of Warcraft or Runescape. In response, schools need to draw clear boundaries and get students outside for recess. We learned that lesson through a year of battling boys to stop playing computer games at recess. One grateful student wrote: "Good job blocking the Video Games. I was getting sick of seeing kids hiding in corners playing WoW [World of Warcraft] instead of having real fun."

Also, we banned computer use at lunch recess, so students would pick up a book in the library or go outside and get covered in wood chips. There is no better picture of balance than a student walking into a class after lunch, draped in wood chips, with a smile on his face.

As reported in the New York Times, research shows that increased physical activity boosts academic performance with greater concentration and focus seen in children (Parker-Pope, February 23, 2009). Those who have spent time teaching middle school boys or who are trying to raise them do not need academic researchers to tell them that if kids cannot have time outside, away from the classroom, it can be a long day for the teacher and the rest of the class. Rainy days are torture for students and teachers. With the push to focus on test scores, many schools curb recess in the belief that students benefit from more time on task in the classroom. However, if you ask a middle school boy what his favorite part of the day is, oftentimes the first and quickest response is "recess." It is heartening to know that there is formal research to support what educators and parents of boys have known through direct experience.

In the words of a Nueva student: "Laptops can be your worst enemy. They make your life much more wired … Whenever there's a chance to engage with people on a bright sunny day, make sure that you do."

This is the ultimate lesson. We live in a wired culture, with Twitter, Facebook, MySpace, and Digg, and we want information at our fingertips, but we also cannot lose sight of the need to teach children how to traverse the technology high wire. A 1-to-1 laptop program, though layered with obstacles and challenges, calls on school communities to engage online culture, come to terms with it, and still keep kids at the core of the mission of schools.

Following the second year of the Nueva 1-to-1 program, the school yearbook included an article entitled "The Laptop Rebellion," which chronicled the storm of protest over the school's AUP at the start of year two of the program. Accompanying the text was a photo montage that showed different iterations of my emotions— from surprise, to anger, to humor—it captured perfectly the roller-coaster experience we have had at Nueva over the course of our two-year experiment.

One of our Nueva eighth grade students, as part of her year-long mentored recital project, which is an in-depth, self-guided exploration, created a series of cartoon strips about different aspects of school life. In one of her illustrations, she outlined the seven different ways to bypass the administrator password, and at the bottom of the illustration she tagged the school motto, "Learn by Doing." She was nervous to show me the cartoon, but when she saw my reaction, which was side-splitting laughter, she relaxed and breathed a sigh of relief. Her father, who witnessed our exchange, commented, "Well, you know you've made it if they [the students] can have a sense of humor about all of this." He is so right.

I was talking with the mother of an eighth grade student, and she proudly shared that she had reached an agreement with her son regarding computer use at home. For every hour he was on the screen, he needed to read for an hour. "That's pretty good, don't you think?" she said. I asked her if he had responded with, "But Mom, I am reading when I'm on the computer." He had not said that to her, but he easily could have, and he would have had a valid point. The amount of reading kids do on the computer is staggering, but it's not the kind my parents used to make me do during the summer months. Instead, kids are fast mastering the skills of skimming, sorting, judging, synthesizing, and manipulating while they jump through screens, clicking on images and icons.

I regularly comb the iTunes App store with my son and marvel at the speed with which he analyzes the potential of various apps. He quickly reads the application summaries provided, plays with the demos, and makes decisions on which free apps to download. He cuts to the chase much better than I can, and he enjoys the "silly" mirror application as much as he grows animated at the Scrabble application, though he also realizes that Scrabble costs $4.99, and he never wants to pay for an application.

According to Chris Anderson, author of *Free: The Future of a Radical Price* (2009), my son is part of the Google Generation:

> They are increasingly unwilling to pay for content and other entertainment, because they have so many free alternatives. They insist on Free not just in price but also in the absence of restrictions: They resist registration barriers, copyright control schemes, and content they can't own. (p. 230)

We rely on my son when we look for a movie on Comcast for family movie night. He zips through the program guide, reads the short film summaries, and then narrows the field to three choices for the family to vote on. My wife, on the other hand, still struggles to scroll through the screen headings, and she is the one who has the miffed expression of a 7-year-old novice piano player when she is pressing the buttons on the remote. She readily hands the reins to our son.

Our 6-year-old daughter is getting in on the game also. She picked up our Flip Video camcorder the other day and started experimenting with it, pressing buttons until she figured out how to record. She is just starting to read, and she recorded herself reading a book. She then listened to herself reading and caught awkward pronunciations and modified her reading and re-recorded herself. She did five takes before she was satisfied that she had gotten it right. Her brother then uploaded her recording to our laptop and edited the movie with iMovie. They added a soundtrack, and we sent the video to my parents.

We even convinced my mother to buy an iPhone. She is of the generation that does not use an ATM machine, so she was terrified. But we reassured her that she would have 24/7 online support from our son, who, via Skype, walks her through the Contacts page of the iPhone. She can't stop giggling at the realization that she is so dependent on her 10-year-old grandson. She already tossed the print manual that she bought at the Apple Store. She said, "The manual is a complete waste. I much prefer the face-to-face guidance

I get on Skype." Even she is thinking about knowledge acquisition in a different way!

This is the potential of the Facebook age. It can transform families, stretch across generations, and allow for innovation and possibility with technology. The Nueva 1-to-1 laptop program forced each and every family and teacher in the school community to come to terms with technology, to make sense of it, to engage with it, and to embrace it for teaching and learning.

The initial days of the laptop program were fraught with fear. Everyone, except the students, of course, gasped at the perils of 1-to-1 learning: the change in school and home culture, the student obsession with games and chats, the new challenges in the classroom for managing student behavior, and the world of cyberbullying at home and at school.

Three years later, the school is humming with possibilities. Grandparents and Special Friends Day, which takes place the day before Thanksgiving each year, is taking on a different feel with technology. Teachers are using Skype to invite grandparents who live in different parts of the country and the globe to participate with their grandchildren. Foreign language teachers are connecting with students in Japan, Spain, and China to video-conference and enhance mastery of the language. Humanities teachers are inventing creative ways to partner with schools in Singapore through ThinkQuest (thinkquest.org), which is free of advertisements and is private. As student e-mails are not required, the school's concerns about privacy and exposing student names on external sites are addressed. Classes are using discussion forums to the point that the school's web developer has had to work out all of the bugs that cropped up as a result of widespread use of these forums.

The remarkably talented science teacher described in the opening is now a Google fellow, working tirelessly with Google to figure out how to harness Google tools to remake science education. One of four teachers selected for this honor, she endured a grueling

chapter 8 | Students and Laptops: Making a Difference?

interview process that asked her to share her thinking aloud as she solved complex programming and real-world problems.

The after-school tech club is preparing for a Linux installfest. Parents will donate old computers, and students will work with experts to wipe the hard drives, fix whatever is broken, clean things up, install Ubuntu Linux on the machines, and then give them away. Ubuntu (www.ubuntu.com) is a community developed, Linux-based operating system with web browser, presentation, document, and spreadsheet software, instant messaging, and more. The Linux installfest is a great way to learn to give back to the community. And, Linux is completely free.

Top Ten Takeaways

There are several takeaways from the Nueva School's experience with rolling out a 1-to-1 laptop program.

1. Listen to the Students

The students are the critical piece of a successful 1-to-1 laptop program. They live with and use the machines each day at school and at home. As Chris Anderson and others have commented, there is a generational, cultural component that schools and families have to come to terms with, and a 1-to-1 laptop program forces the issue to surface. There is no hiding. Students need to have a voice in creating and shaping acceptable use policies (AUPs) at school and media guidelines at home. Without student input, school communities attempting to start a 1-to-1 program will have a very rocky ride, as the Nueva School learned. Also, schools need to develop courses—like programming and space art, for example—that grow out of students' interests and passions. This will captivate students and redirect their interest in technology toward productive ends.

2. Involve, Prepare, and Educate Parents

The parent community has to understand the rationale for a switch to a 1-to-1 laptop program and how giving a laptop to every student enhances teaching and learning. If steps are not taken to prepare parents for the transition to having a laptop in their homes, there is significant pushback, resistance, and even resentment. Also, schools need to take the time to celebrate and advertise curricular achievements, in the form of curriculum culmination evenings where student media creations are on display, or communicate technology achievements in newsletters to parents. Otherwise, schools run the risk of standing on the backs of their heels as they try to sort through student transgressions with laptops, and parents learn about all that can go wrong with technology.

3. Create Professional Development Opportunities for Teachers

Teacher professional development is key. A 1-to-1 laptop program places the need for curricular change on the table. Schools need to devote precious professional development dollars to technology training with the right technology leaders. Alan November fit the Nueva community perfectly. His iconoclastic, innovative, bold approaches resonated for Nueva teachers, and his summer conference served as the perfect outlet for many of our teachers to find and implement fresh approaches with technology. Earmarking staff meeting time for technology education is a must. Teachers need time to digest new tools and to have time with colleagues to discuss, experiment with, and ultimately deploy these new tools. Finally, schools need to cultivate a culture of risk-taking and innovation with technology and move away from fear-based approaches that can hamstring experimentation with technology in the classroom. In addition, teacher evaluation proved to be another key component of fostering teacher growth with technology. Bringing teams of teachers together to observe colleagues in action, coupled with the opportunity to guide the teacher being evaluated by providing encouragement to utilize technology more fully, helped to propel the laptop program.

4. Don't Go It Alone

Early on in year one of the 1-to-1 laptop program at Nueva, we realized that we needed to speak with experts. We did not hesitate to reach out for help, and Common Sense Media played a key role in helping us figure out how to move forward with parents. Our relations with Common Sense Media deepened, and they came to Nueva to speak to parents. Nueva now has a formal partnership with Common Sense Media and is piloting its curricular materials, which will soon extend to schools around the country. Others who helped us include Erin Reilly of New Media Literacies, cybersafety expert Steve DeWarns, and Alan November.

5. Be Flexible

A 1-to-1 laptop program brings surprises and unforeseen situations. Schools need to know that not knowing how to handle a situation is okay, but they need to be flexible enough to work with students, parents, and teachers to develop solutions together. Each new situation is an opportunity to learn, and given the dizzying pace of change in today's media, there is simply no way to stay ahead of the students. Also, schools need to have a flexible web developer who can customize solutions based on the needs of students and teachers. The last thing schools should do is lock in on a system that cannot be modified, whether the desired change is to create a new calendar function on the website or even to introduce the prototype of an internal chat program for students.

6. Stay the Course

There were moments when we wanted to abandon the 1-to-1 laptop program, especially during year one. The culture clash between students and adults was at its sharpest point, and many adults felt overwhelmed and powerless to keep the program moving forward. We constantly had to take the long view and look at the evolution of the program over time. It would have been easy and convenient to push pause and to reevaluate and reconfigure the program, at the loss of forward progress. In conversations with outside experts and organizations, we received assurances that the bumps we were experiencing were part of the natural course of a change of culture. The inspiration provided by organizations like IDEO kept the school hopeful in its charge to transform teaching and learning with laptops.

7. Maintain Balance

It is easy to get swept up in fear when students are handed school-issued laptops. Schools must maintain a balance between keeping students safe at school with computers and introducing the imaginative, creative possibilities that computers generate. Also, schools must remain mindful that it is essential to steer students toward physical play outdoors, even when students feel the pull to play on their laptops.

8. Remember That Kids Are Kids, and They Need Guidance

Renowned Harvard University educator Howard Gardner has likened the Internet to the Wild West, and a 1-to-1 laptop program gives students a wider entry into this largely uncharted territory. Students will make mistakes, test boundaries, and need guidance from their teachers and parents. Technology is a different tool, for sure, one with great possibility, but teachers and parents need to remember to take time to recognize and teach the ethical lessons that arise with a 1-to-1 laptop program. Embedding these lessons in the "core" curriculum is a must, whether this comes in the form of a boot-up camp day, like the one Nueva instituted, or through advisory programs and media literacy or computer classes.

9. Keep Learning with Students

Technology is moving at lightning speed, and school communities need to be open to learning about the latest tools along with students. Parents and teachers set the tone through their willingness to sit next to and learn from students. The role of the teacher has changed, and school communities need to grow comfortable with these changing roles. Students can and should be placed in teaching roles with technology.

10. Overcome Fears

Wikipedia describes Web 2.0 this way:

> [Web 2.0] is commonly associated with web applications that facilitate interactive information sharing, interoperability, user-centered design, and collaboration on the World Wide Web. Examples of Web 2.0 include web-based communities, hosted services, web applications, social-networking sites, video-sharing sites, wikis, blogs, mashups, and folksonomies [collaborative indexing].

Well, Web 2.0 has become iSchool 2.0, and school communities need to leverage these tools to enhance teaching and learning. Students are at the hub of Web 2.0 activity, and they want to learn in schools that use these tools. Schools have to come to terms with their fear of Web 2.0 and embrace their transformation into iSchools 2.0.

Conclusion

The Nueva School's experience with 1-to-1 laptop learning serves as both a cautionary and inspiring tale for school communities considering the move to 1-to-1 laptop learning. Nueva never stands still and is always on the hunt for the next new thing. "Free" is the next frontier to cross with 1-to-1 laptop learning. Schools in Brazil are moving in this direction, with over 350,000 Linux-operated machines heading into municipal schools. According to Chris Anderson in *Free: The Future of a Radical Price* (2009), Brazil is fast becoming a world leader in the area of open source, which is computer software where the source code is freely available. Anderson writes:

> Brazil built the first ATM based on Linux. The prime directive of the Federal Institute for Information Technology is to promote the adoption of free software throughout the government and the nation. Ministries and schools are migrating their offices to open source systems. And within the government's digital inclusion programs—aimed at bringing computer access to the 80% of Brazilians who have none—Linux is the rule. (p. 207)

Open source programming languages like Python may soon enter school curricula, along with courses in electronic circuitry. Open source image-editing software like Gimp may soon replace the expensive iPhoto application. And, open source graphics-editing software like Inkscape may make pricey applications like Adobe Illustrator obsolete.

Regardless of the direction technology takes, the Nueva School will be there to meet it with open arms, ready and willing to embrace innovation, with full knowledge that "if you're not falling down every now and again, it's a sign that you're not doing anything innovative," as Woody Allen likes to say.